DR ALEX GEORGE

A BetteR DAy

illustrated by
The Boy Fitz Hammond

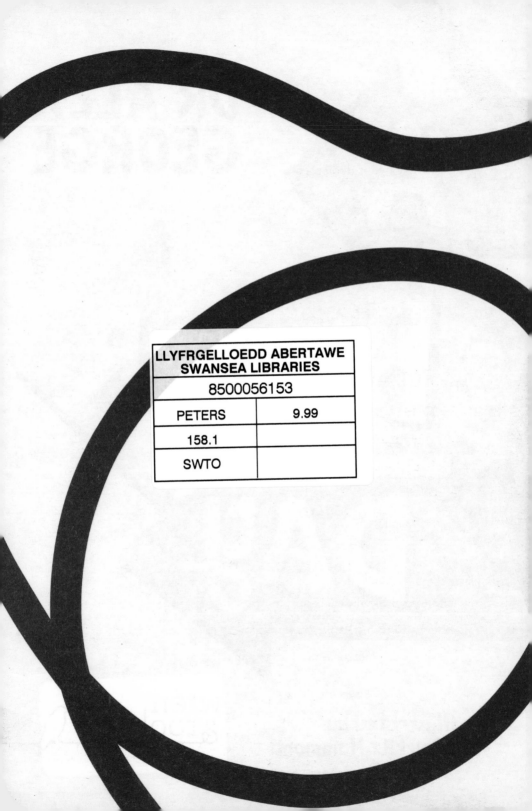

This book is dedicated to Mam, Dad, Elliott and Llŷr.

'Life throws us into the deep end at times, however, with the help of family and friends, we overcome even the most seemingly insurmountable challenges.'

Thank you for always being there for me, through thick and thin. Thank you for believing in me, no matter what. I love you.

CONTENTS

INTRODUCTION

My secret superpower!

I'm Alex, and worry is my middle name. At least it should have been when I was at school. From the moment I woke up each day, I could always find something to fret about. It was as if I had a special place inside my mind where I could stew about things so badly it kept me awake at night.

Mostly I worried about life at school. In particular, I got it into my head that all my teachers secretly hated me. In maths and English, through science, geography, history and even PE, I marked myself down as the pupil nobody particularly wanted to teach.

I wasn't badly behaved. In fact, I worked *really* hard. I didn't know it at the time, but I was dyslexic. It meant I struggled with reading and writing, which just added to my worries. It knocked my self-confidence and wrongly left me feeling like I just wasn't as smart as my classmates. I worried that my teachers would think I was being lazy, when in reality my brain was just wired slightly differently to make sense of things like spelling. What's more, no teacher showed any evidence that they disliked me. Still, that didn't stop me from thinking that they were all just waiting for me to do something wrong.

'*Alex George!*' I imagined one would yell from the front if it all kicked off. '*Who gave you permission to glance out the window? That's it! I've had enough! If you can't pay attention properly in my class, then you're good for nothing but failure for the rest of your life! Get out and don't come back! Ever!*'

I know. Overdramatic or what? I told you I was a world-class worrier.

Just me?

To make things harder on myself, I decided that nobody else shared the same worries. My friends never seemed concerned that the teachers might secretly have their name on a list of pupils they never wanted to see again. If anyone got told off for talking in class or answered a question wrongly, they didn't react as if it had just ruined their whole term. They just shrugged it off and got on with their school day. I was alone, it seemed, in believing that I had to be on my best behaviour to avoid the teachers turning on me. Over time, it made me feel miserable. My worries were constantly humming away in the background of my life. I found them impossible to switch off.

Not once did I let my parents know what was on my mind. I was quite good at hiding it from them and pretending that everything was just fine. But it didn't make my worries any easier to carry around with me. If anything, it just made me feel cut off from help and support, and left me lying awake at night fretting about what the next day might have in store. I was alone in believing that

my teachers secretly belonged to the Alex Is a Terrible Person Club, and it was just something I had to live with. It would be fine, but only as long as I avoided slipping up, which would be the opportunity any of them needed to stop pretending they liked me.

Worst moment ever!

'That's all for today, class,' said my chemistry teacher on the day I was forced to face my worst fears. 'Please leave your homework on my table on your way out.'

I heard the instruction clearly. But instead of reaching for my bag like everyone else, I just forgot to blink and breathe. *Homework?* I thought to myself in a panic. I had made a note to do it. I just thought this one was due later in the week.

'I haven't even started it yet!' I admitted to a friend as everyone rose from their desks. 'What am I going to do?' My friend just shrugged like it wasn't his problem. To be fair, he'd done his homework on time. He didn't have anything to worry about. Not like me. Just then, it felt like the entire world had stopped turning.

With no homework to hand in, I prepared to find myself in big trouble. *My teacher will be furious*, I thought to myself as I broke into a cold sweat. I'd face detention and if the head was having a bad day, maybe I'd even be expelled from the school! Then I'd never be able to take my exams, which meant my dreams of going to medical school and becoming a doctor would come crashing down. To make things worse, my parents would think I was a huge disappointment. I'd probably have to leave home. Thanks to this one small mistake, I convinced myself, I was destined to live the rest of my life as a total loser.

As I gathered my things, preparing to confess all to my teacher, it felt like my entire future lay in ruins. Just then, if the ground had opened up beneath my feet and swallowed me whole, it might have been a better option.

'What's on your mind, Alex?' The teacher was packing up to move on to his next lesson. He barely glanced at me as I approached his desk. I felt a knot form in my stomach.

'Well, erm . . . the thing is . . .' As I tried to get my excuses out, the knot began to tighten. I paused, feeling dizzy and sick, which is when he looked up as if my time had just run out. *'I haven't done my homework!'* I blurted, and that knot felt like it snapped inside me. 'I'm sorry. I just forgot.'

My teacher nodded and then collected the books that my classmates had just handed in. 'Can you get it done for me by tomorrow?' he asked.

It took a moment for my brain to register that he hadn't just ordered me to disappear into the wilderness and spend the next twenty years alone reflecting on where I had gone wrong. He'd just given me a little extension on my homework deadline.

'Um . . . yes,' I said, shocked at his response. 'I can do that.'

'Good.' He smiled before turning for the door. 'Enjoy the rest of your day, Alex.'

'You too, sir,' I called after him eventually, but by then he was gone.

Time to change

That moment will always stay with me. It proved to be a turning point in how I managed my worries. Until then, I had let them control me. I had become a master in finding something to fret about, even if there was no reason for it. For me, everything changed when my chemistry teacher shrugged off the fact that I'd forgotten to do my homework and then gave me an opportunity to catch up. Without realising it, he'd shown me that I'd turned a minor concern into a massive problem without any good reason.

On the way home, as I reflected on my situation, I realised that I had become very good at fuelling my worries with all sorts of unrealistic fears. Nobody got expelled for being late with their homework once. I had no evidence to seriously think that would happen. In the same way, if I really thought about it, no teacher had shown any sign of disliking me. I was well behaved, helpful and polite (most of the time). Like most kids my age, I could also be a little forgetful, as my late homework had shown. That didn't make me bad or doomed to life as a hermit because the whole world hated me. I just needed to complete a multiple-choice quiz about chemistry that evening and all would be well.

So that night, having completed my late homework, I struck a deal with myself. I had let my worries control my life for long enough, and now it was time for that to change. I knew I couldn't just stop fretting about things. In fact, I decided that a little worry was a healthy thing. It showed I was sensitive to others and keen to do the right thing, and there was nothing wrong with that.

Not all superheroes wear their pants on the outside

Changing my relationship with worry was a small step, but it led to a giant leap in my approach to life. I still got concerned about stuff. It's only natural, after all. But instead of letting my worries take charge of me, I started using them to my advantage.

By tuning into how I was feeling and learning to talk about what was on my mind, I turned my worries into what sometimes felt like a personal superpower. OK, so I couldn't leap off tall buildings or fly. My new ability didn't exactly qualify me to wear a caped outfit with my pants on the outside, but it felt pretty special to me.

Quite simply, I had the ability to take a negative thought and transform it into a positive one. Like all new superheroes, it took me a while to control my powers and not let a little concern turn into a major crisis. With practice, however, I learned that if my worry senses started tingling, I could use it as an opportunity to get things done in good time.

As an ordinary, sensitive kid, discovering that I could tap into my mind in this way was a game-changer. If tests – which could feel like my arch-enemy – were looming, I learned that the best thing I could do was take a deep breath, sit down and go through the subject I needed to cover. It was better than feeling overwhelmed or finding distractions to avoid spending time with my schoolbooks. That wouldn't make my worries go away. It just made them worse. By acting positively and defeating my worry head on, I discovered that good things could happen, and this really helped me through my years at school. As an older student, not only could I enjoy the breaks in the revision plans I set up to help me study, but it also meant I was prepared – and calm – when it came to turning over the papers in the exam hall.

This didn't happen overnight. It took time for me to make friends with my ability to worry. First, I had to understand what caused it, and eventually I realised it came down to a fear of disappointing people. I never liked to let anyone down, and somehow I had let that become a monster in my mind. It got so bad that I made every effort to be perfect, which was both exhausting and unrealistic. Once I recognised this and realised that although I can't control what other people think of me, I can control how I feel about myself, my worries became easier to deal with. I didn't try to stamp them out. I just tried to turn what could feel like a negative thought into a positive opportunity.

'what's the worst that can happen?' I'll often ask myself.

This question helped me burst the balloon of worry that built up every time I started fretting. I realised that as long as I did my best to prepare for whatever challenge I was facing, even if the worst happened, I could handle it. This gave me the confidence to give it my best shot. Whether I was about to take an exam, meeting new people or hoping to join a game of football with friends (even though I'm the least talented player in human history!), it meant I could hold my head high and just go for it.

If anything, my secret superpower has encouraged me to step out of my comfort zone. I've learned that when I'm in an unfamiliar environment – and there's a chance I might not succeed the first time I try something – I rise to the challenge and learn things about myself in the process. It's how I stepped up to live my dream of becoming a doctor, and it's how I took part in one of the world's best-known TV reality shows . . . *Love Island.*

Sometimes I still have bad worry days. None of us lead completely calm and happy lives, after all. Looking back at my time at school, I realise now that lots of people had worries. The fact is, worrying is something we all experience to some degree, whether it's about making friends or falling out with people, the future, or problems at home, school and everything in between. Some people also struggle with other emotions that can feel overwhelming, such as:

sadness   Anger

Loneliness   Frustration

It's only when I started to talk with others, and we shared our experiences, that I recognised it's all part of being human and that I wasn't alone.

I like to think of life as a journey, because everyone has ups, downs, detours and wrong turns. But there are always ways to get things heading in the right direction, see the positives and look towards the future with optimism. After being faced with an obstacle, I frequently say to myself the simple word 'onwards'. Because no matter how bad things feel right now, there is always hope for a better day.

Let's light up our lives

This book is about mental wellness. We're talking about the thoughts, feelings and actions that help us to make sense of ourselves and the world around us. It's easy to think of mental health in terms of just problems, or something that needs to be fixed. I want us to think differently. It's not all about people looking sad with a rain cloud looming over their heads. It's also about feeling happy, relaxed and able to deal with any situation life throws at us. Mental health can mean lots of things, and by learning to connect with what's going on inside our minds, we can turn it into a force for good.

I didn't exactly enjoy my early brush with difficult feelings like worry, but with the right tools and understanding, I learned how to manage it and even use it to my advantage. In the same way, once I realised that my challenges with reading and writing were down to a recognised learning difficulty called dyslexia, I received all kinds of tips, help and support that made things easier. Rather than struggling on my own, feeling like there was something wrong with me, I found the confidence to express myself to the best of my abilities – not only on paper but in everyday life!

Since qualifying as a doctor, I've spent a great deal of time working in a hospital. There, I see young people every day who are struggling with mental health issues. It could be anything from depression or despair to anxiety or eating disorders, all of which we'll cover later. Often, these young people feel like nothing can be done. From my experience with worries and learning difficulties, I know how easy it is to think like this. In every case, however, help and support is always available.

What's more, it can turn lives around. I've always been passionate about giving young people the tools they need to manage or overcome any challenge with their mental health, and now I'm on a mission to make those tools available to everyone.

As the Youth Mental Health Ambassador appointed by the Prime Minister, I'm determined to make a change for the better. None of us are born with an instruction manual that shows how to keep our minds in good shape. We have to get to grips with it as we grow up, and that can be challenging. At the same time, I learned from experience that we don't have to do this alone. Help and advice is always out there for us all, and not just for those moments when we're finding life tough. I passionately believe that the sooner we make sense of our thoughts and feelings, the better equipped we'll be to make the most of our lives, which is why I've written this book. I want to make mental wellness something to celebrate, and that begins by turning the page.

PART ONE

MENTAL WELLNESS AND ME (AND THAT MEANS YOU!)

CHAPTER 1

PULLING THE LEVERS IN YOUR MIND

When we talk about getting into shape, most of us think about physical fitness. At school we have PE teachers constantly reminding us to be active for at least an hour per day. And when we go home, we hear about the importance of a balanced diet.

You see, the reminders and importance of keeping physically healthy are all around us. We know that being fit will keep our muscles strong and our lungs and hearts in good working order. And when it comes to running for the bus, keeping fit might even mean we'll be able to catch it, or at least get close enough so that the driver can catch a glimpse of our desperate faces and stop.

But even without these small victories, keeping fit can be so much fun. Some of us enjoy being active without putting much thought into it. Others find fulfilment in dedicating themselves to achieving top levels of fitness or performance. We only have to look at Team GB Olympians, such as diver Tom Daley and sprinter Dina Asher-Smith, to recognise that dedication can bring rewards that go beyond any trophy or medal. But even if it's just playground games when we're little, taking part in a team sport or heading out for a walk with the dog, we all know how good it can feel to get some fresh air and keep our bodies in good working order.

So my question is, why don't we pay as much care and attention to our minds as we do to our bodies?

We're talking about that space inside our heads where we do all our thinking. It shapes what kind of mood we're in and how we feel about ourselves. Sometimes we call it a *mental* space. It isn't something we can see when we stand in front of a mirror, and yet our mental health is just as important as keeping physically fit. The two are so connected that unless we take care of one, the other can suffer. If we're feeling down, for example, it's very easy to find we don't have much enthusiasm for being active or eating properly. In the same way, if we lead physically unhealthy lifestyles, we can fall into negative ways of thinking about ourselves.

Physical and mental health both play a vital role in helping us to live happy, fulfilling and rewarding lives. By understanding how the mind works and valuing mental wellness in the same way we do physical fitness, we can learn how to keep our bodies in good working order – inside and out – while setting ourselves up to make the most of life in every way.

Our mind is just as important as our heart or lungs, and yet it won't show up on a scan. Unlike our vital organs, the mind is not a physical part of the body. It's just a word we give to the way our brains process thoughts, moods and feelings (which we can also sometimes call *emotions*). To make sense of what we're talking about here, let's imagine a series of levers. Each one represents a different emotion, from happiness and joy to love and sadness, from confidence and anger to shyness and stress. I like to think each lever has a label so we don't get confused. Nobody wants to accidentally look disgusted when presented with their favourite cake, or to scream when they're actually feeling calm and content. Luckily, our minds know how to work these levers without us really thinking about it. Phew! This is welcome news, because when we consider the huge range of feelings we can experience, we're talking about a LOT of levers. In short, the human mind is pretty smart.

What's more, each lever is constantly adjusting itself as we live our lives. Walk into a surprise birthday party and our happiness lever might tilt to full power for a while. In the same way, opening up a tin of chocolates to discover someone's had the last one could cause our annoyance lever to briefly click forward by a notch. In fact, at any moment in time, every single lever will be activated to some degree – and will keep adjusting according to what's going on with us. Even if we don't feel annoyed, that lever will still be primed to take over when we fall off our bike and scratch the frame.

Quite simply, our levers are always moving backwards and forwards, and in a way that's unique to each and every one of us. If I visit an amusement park with my friend but she chooses not to ride the rollercoaster with me, chances are *my* fear and excitement levers are going to be tested to the max.

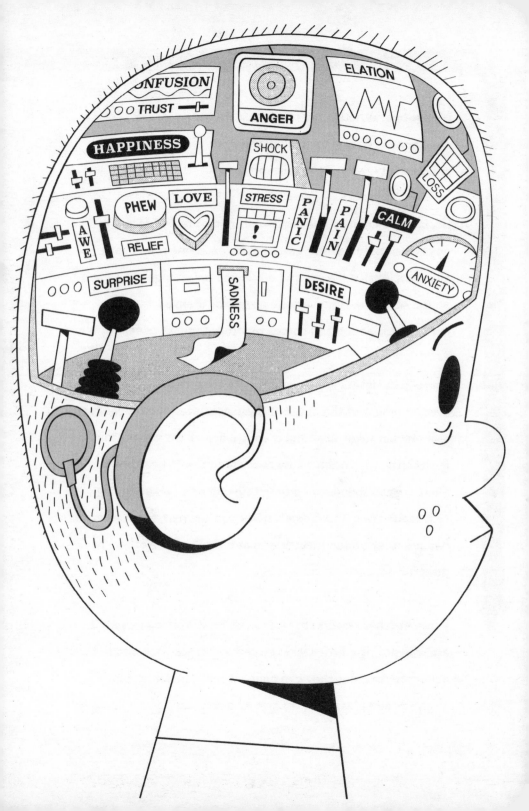

Meanwhile, although my friend is scared of rides, after seeing me dizzy and having to remind myself to blink, *her* joy and amusement levers might shift into gear.

So, in any instant, our levers are primed to feel all sorts of emotions, moving from fear to joy to excitement and back again. We're all different and our levers will change depending on the situation. But every single one of them performs an important function and comes together to make us feel whole.

These many levers are constantly adjusting to see us through every moment of the day, but there are times when it can feel as if one has taken over and is controlling all the others. This is often the case when we feel very sad or even heartbroken. Then, we can spend a long time thinking we're always going to feel the same way. Sometimes it can seem as if that lever has got stuck on full throttle and as a result all the others have powered down.

In reality, those levers that we haven't felt working in a while are still moving a little bit. They can also creak back into full action. Sometimes they can do it without assistance, but it's always good to learn how to give a helping hand – like oiling up squeaky or stiff metal levers to help them move more smoothly. As we'll explore later, this begins by understanding what role each lever plays, and then asking why it doesn't feel like it's functioning normally. Whether it's a quick and easy do-it-yourself fix or needs the aid of a health professional, help is always out there. Our emotions are constantly working together to enable us to make sense of ourselves and our place in the world, but sometimes we just need that extra support from people who care for us to get all the levers moving nicely.

These levers don't actually exist, of course. We're not robots, but the mind can be compared to a supercomputer. Why? Because it processes thoughts and feelings thousands of times each day. By using these imaginary levers to visualise how the mind works, we can begin to understand what an important role it plays in our lives. Some might even say that it's this wonderful, complex thing inside our heads that really makes us human.

Robots vs humans

When people talk about mental wellness, or good mental health, it's easy to think they must be imagining a mind in which the happy lever is doing all the work. Now wouldn't that

be lovely! But life isn't that simple. In some ways it would be very dull – and weird – if we all went about with endless grins on our faces and not a care in the world. If I woke up one day to find everyone smiling at me, I'd think I was in some kind of computer simulation. It just wouldn't feel real. And I'd probably end up running for the hills trying to escape the smiling robots!

We lead complex, challenging and sometimes difficult lives, and our emotions are designed to reflect that. Nobody wants to feel angry or frustrated, but these feelings are both important and completely natural. They serve as a pressure release when things don't go our way – a bit like a boiling kettle. If we didn't yell or shake our fists at the skies every now and then, we'd never get those feelings out of our system. We'd just spend our whole time quietly fuming. It also means when the good times follow, we can truly appreciate them.

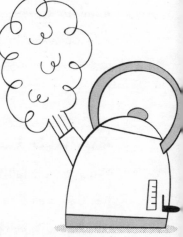

Sometimes feelings can seem unwanted, whether it's emotions like sadness, embarrassment or even feeling grumpy and fed up for no reason. It can also be tiring carrying some of these tougher feelings around, and we might sometimes wish we could just power down our emotions, like machines. That's when we need to remind ourselves that being human is a better option. Why? Well, even though some feelings can be hard to handle, they all play a vital role in helping us to make sense of our world.

If we feel comfortable with the full range of our feelings, and not just the positive ones, we're less likely to bottle up difficult emotions and hope they go away. We can begin to recognise why they're being triggered and be better prepared to deal with them constructively. Luckily, we can do this in all sorts of different ways, depending on what works for us, and you will find plenty of suggestions in this book.

But remember, we are all on a different journey when it comes to our mental wellness. So although some people might go for a run, because they find exercise helps to clear their heads, others might put their feelings into words by opening up to someone they trust, to get the advice, support and help they deserve. Sometimes even just recognising that today is not your day, and that you need to take a break or be kind to yourself, is all you need to feel a little better and give yourself energy for tomorrow. This is what we mean by good mental health, or mental wellness. It's about getting in touch with what's going on inside our minds, which is what this book is all about.

IT'S **OK** IF TODAY IS NOT YOUR DAY. ♥

We all owe it to ourselves to take care of our mental health. And lucky for you, unlike our physical fitness, we don't have to break into a sweat to get our minds into good shape. There are workouts we can do in our heads to make us mentally fit and strong enough to deal with whatever life throws at us. But mental strength isn't about muscle power. It's about identifying and managing any feelings we experience and reaching out when we need a helping hand. What's more, these are skills that are easy to master. Honestly, if I can learn to make good use of them, anyone can! So let's look at how we can start helping ourselves as well as providing support for other people.

CHAPTER 2

IT'S (REALLY) GOOD TO TALK

OK, so we learn how to verbalise our thoughts at an early age, going from the infant cry to speaking in full sentences. Some of us never stop talking (you must know that chatty student in class – or maybe it's you?), and others prefer to stay a bit more on the quiet side. Whichever end of the chatty spectrum we sit on, I think we can still all agree that communication is a key part of life. So why is it that when it comes to talking about feelings and tricky emotions, many of us find it hard to put our innermost thoughts into words?

Well, there are lots of different reasons why we don't find it easy to speak up, especially when it comes to talking about mental health. We may think:

We're bringing the mood down by mentioning it in conversation

Admitting that we're not coping is somehow a sign that we've let ourselves down

The fact is, most of these barriers are walls that we've built up in our minds and they couldn't be further from the truth. Instead they muzzle us from ever speaking and cause us to bottle up feelings, which can be harmful.

I'll be the first to admit that being able to talk openly about our emotional lives takes courage. If anything, it's a sign of strength, and while it might seem daunting for some, in every case people feel better for voicing what's going on inside their minds.

People might make a big deal and treat us differently

People won't understand and might judge us, or they might make fun of or bully us

we haven't made sense of what our feelings are yet and so we think, 'what's the point?'

Here are a few tips to help us start talking:

☆ **Learn to open up.** It can be tough when we've never really done it before. It can feel very personal, and make us feel vulnerable and bare, which is why many people choose to say nothing. Practise talking about feelings. It might feel weird to begin with, but once you get the hang of it, you'll be so glad you took that first step.

☆ **Be ready to listen.** As well as learning how to ask for help, we need to know when to listen. If someone turns to us for support, the most effective thing we can do is allow them to talk and enable them to feel heard. Most of the time people just want an ear to listen. It's also important to know where to direct someone to find help – there are some resources in the Help Yourself section on page 215, which would be a good place to look.

☆ **Trust is key.** It takes courage to talk honestly about our mental health. What matters is that we feel safe when we open up, and this comes down to trust. Everyone is different, of course. Some people prefer to talk to a family member or close friend. Others feel more comfortable confiding in their doctor, a nurse, a school counsellor or even anonymously via a helpline by email, chat, text or phone.

⭐ **Don't wait for a crisis.** We know how to talk about a range of topics for everyday conversations. Opening up about our emotions should be no different to talking about homework or what we had for dinner last night. Let's make mental wellness a subject we can chat about at any time. We all experience feelings, after all, and if we can feed that into our everyday chats then we're more likely to catch any minor concerns before they turn into something bigger.

Asking for help

It's one thing for us to recognise the importance of talking about our feelings and having the courage to open up, but actually putting this into practice, and specifically asking for *help*, can be a challenge for many people, especially at a difficult emotional time.

When I was at school and worried that every teacher hated me, it seemed like, at the same time, my own face had turned against me. Spots (or acne) are a fact of teenage life for so many, and I seemed to have them bad. It was like playing *and* failing at a game of Whac-A-Mole, because as soon as one spot looked like it was retreating from angry redness, a new spot or even two would appear. Just looking in the mirror could leave me feeling very low.

It rocked my confidence, and for a long time, I just bottled up my feelings about it. Eventually, I spoke to my mum and she encouraged me to check in with my doctor, who prescribed a course of treatment.

Though I had to sit in the doctor's office feeling embarrassed and helpless, the GP reassured me that it is something every teenager goes through, and the treatment worked wonders. But most of all, it was the chance to get the subject out into the open that made me feel so much better.

When we've got a problem, we can often feel like we don't want to trouble anyone by sharing it. People lead busy lives, after all. Why would we want to add to that by admitting we're not coping?

The simple response to anyone reluctant to speak up and ask for help is that people who care for us will always want to help. It's human nature. Just think about how we would react if someone we know turned to us. Even if we aren't sure how to help, we can all listen. Often, this is the most effective thing we can offer, along with reminding someone that we'll stand by them while they get the right support.

Although we're all different and have our own ways of coping and dealing with our emotions (I've certainly tried and tested a few), I have put together a simple self-help toolkit to help you get started. It's made up of something called Lifelines, which are easy to use and are designed to help us all.

What are Lifelines?

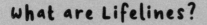

Lifelines are effective ways to open up and seek the help and support we deserve. They can take many forms. They can help us to feel like we're not alone, and we can lean on them when feelings become hard to handle – whether we're in a moment of crisis or just feel like we need to process our thoughts. They help us take the first step towards getting to grips with the issue. Let's look at some of the best examples of Lifelines:

Write your feelings down. A piece of paper and a pencil, or even a notetaking app on our phone, can help us to make sense of what's going on inside our minds. Writing is a great way to express ourselves. It could just be a couple of sentences, or a few pages, or more. Whatever feels right, putting feelings into words helps us to 'see' the problem more clearly. It may not bring instant results, but even just admitting that we're not coping can be the first step towards making sense of a situation.

Turn to friends, family or a responsible adult. What matters most is that we choose to talk to someone we trust who will simply listen without judging us. This could be a friend or family member, or it could be a responsible adult outside of our home or circle of friends. They will listen and help us to decide on the most appropriate course of action that puts our mental welfare first.

It's worth remembering that only a medical health professional – such as a doctor – can diagnose a mental health disorder and provide an appropriate treatment plan too. This begins by making an appointment at our local doctor's surgery, which can be done alone or with the help of a parent or carer. Your conversation with a doctor will be kept confidential unless you are at risk of harm.

When you have decided who to turn to, try thinking about the following:

Choose a good moment. When opening up to a family member or friend, find a time when things are quiet and calm – a moment when no one is in a rush to get somewhere or distracted by what's on TV. You might even find it easier to talk when you're in the car or walking side-by-side. At times like this, you tend to naturally look forward, instead of looking directly at one another, which can feel less intense.

Be prepared to ask again. If you ask for help but don't get what you're looking for, simply regroup and speak up elsewhere. Sometimes people just don't understand or don't feel equipped to provide support. Consider it a learning experience and look elsewhere. Asking for help is not a one-shot opportunity. Keep asking until you are heard.

Focus on the positives. Remember, there are lots of positives to reaching out. Just putting feelings into words can help to ease some stress and emotional pressure. It has to be better than bottling it up, which can just make things seem worse. Even if it doesn't sort the problem straight away, confiding in someone we trust means we're not facing it alone.

What's more, at a time when we can feel like nobody will understand what we're facing, talking is the surest way to learn

that others have been through similar experiences and come out feeling stronger.

Help yourself. At the back of this book, I've put together a big list of places, spaces, charities and helplines dedicated to providing support and advice to young people about all mental health issues. It's just one more way that we can place positive mental wellness at the centre of our lives.

As you go through the different mental health subjects covered in this book, you'll notice I've  stamped loads of pages with these Lifelines. You've been warned, I will be talking about these Lifelines a LOT, but only because they're such effective and simple tools that make a huge difference.

Heads up! Here's what's in store . . .

The first stop on our journey into the world of mental health begins with common feelings that can shape our daily lives. In particular, we'll look at states of mind we sometimes think of as unwelcome, such as worry and anxiety and sadness.

As we'll discover, all feelings play an important role in our lives. What matters is that we know how to manage them. We could be talking about those days when we just feel flat, on edge or just a bit meh. Maybe we've fallen out with a friend, or find we've missed out on an invite to a party, or just got out of bed and have no energy. They're the kind of days we want to skip or forget, and that can overshadow all the good things going on.

And if you have lots of these days, there might be something bigger going on that you need some extra support with. So let's explore what can seem like negative, difficult or challenging emotions, and then set out ways to process them, so that no matter what, you can look towards a better day – every day.

Ready for a mental workout?

Here we go . . .

PART TWO

AN INSIDE GUIDE TO THE MIND

CHAPTER 3

A MENTAL WORKOUT—DEFEATING ANXIETY

I like going to the gym. It's my happy place, which might sound weird but it's true! As part of my routine, I take myself there to work out, keep fit and stay healthy. But when I first started going to the gym, I was *completely* clueless. I remember walking into a room full of people who looked like total pros hitting the machines, lifting huge weights and stretching out on their yoga mats, and I thought, *I might just walk straight back out again.*

But I took a deep breath and asked the instructor to show me what to do. I couldn't just wing it. I needed to learn to use the equipment without putting myself or the other gym users in danger. Soon enough, I had worked out how to jump on the running machine without it sending me flying across the room, and I had figured out the technique for lifting a dumb-bell without dropping it on my foot. Slowly, the weights and exercise machines became useful tools that helped me to make the most of my gym sessions.

As we discussed in chapter 1, our mental health is just as important as our physical health. But while people go to the gym to get physical, we can work on our mental fitness at any time and place. Even so, our minds can still feel weirdly unfamiliar the first time we pause to think about what's actually going on in there. So think of me as the instructor who shows new members around. We're talking about a space that has a lot to offer, but it can be hard to know where to begin. By taking a tour inside the mind, we can get familiar with it and see it as a comfortable place that works for us all. Plus,

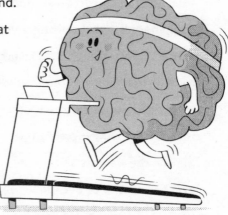

we can learn which tools will help us make it stronger, more flexible and ready for all the complex feelings that life can throw our way.

On the tour we'll pick apart common feelings we often find hard to handle, which can also be a factor when we consider the relationship we have with our bodies, our identity and the bonds we have with others. We'll ask what can trigger these feelings and allow them to take hold.

If someone is giving us a hard time at school, for example – which is also known as bullying – it can dent our self-confidence. Even if we're just feeling picked on, it's not OK and it can affect other areas of our lives, leaving us feeling alone and even worthless. Sometimes we might even lose sight of the fact that we are victims of bullying, and blame ourselves for feeling low rather than speaking up to stamp it out. There are all sorts of reasons why we might find ourselves living with difficult feelings without recognising what's behind them. By learning to talk about them here, we stand a good chance of making those connections and then tackling the cause.

We can also often slip into a state of mind that leaves us unhappy without realising what's happening. It can just seem like our feelings are working against us. That's when we can wrongly think that nothing will improve the situation. When my worries ruled my life, for example, and left me in fear of doing something wrong, I resigned myself to feeling stressed, anxious and often just miserable. It was only when I forgot about my homework, and my teacher cheerily gave me an extension to do it, that I saw light at the end of the tunnel. I started to think about what was behind my worries, and then realised I could do something about them. With this growing awareness, my life became more relaxed, enjoyable and fulfilling. It was my first experience of taking responsibility for my mental health. It took a while for me to sort things out, but that could only happen once I realised that I had the power to make positive changes.

The fact is, emotions can be managed. It's not a question of stamping them out or locking them away, which isn't effective or healthy. It's about understanding what's causing difficult feelings to take shape and then figuring out ways to bring them under control.

What's even better is that with this outlook, we can set up an action plan to tackle any mental health issue. On this tour I want us all to feel empowered. Even if these issues don't affect us right now, learning to recognise the signs – as well as knowing how to address them – can only help us live our lives to the full. It's normal to face challenging moments, now or in the future. The good news is that help for any mental health issue is always out there. It's just a question of asking, and soon we'll discover that we're never alone.

THERE IS ALWAYS HOPE OF A BETTER DAY.

How to ace anxiety and worry

Ah yes, it's the first stop on our tour and we've come back to my familiar foe – worry. If we stop to think about worry, it serves a useful purpose. A little worry goes a long way when it comes to crossing the road safely. It's what prompts us to look left and right, after all. In the same way, most of us tend not to leave the bath tap running while we take a nap. Why not? Because it's only natural that we worry about what might happen if we make poor choices.

A worry-free world might sound like a wonderful place to be, but the good times wouldn't last long. Personally, I have better things to do than deal with soaking wet floors and taking my life in my hands every time I cross a road. Looking at worry in this light, we can see that it plays a vital role in our lives. But we have to avoid it getting out of control and, speaking as a former world-class worrier, we need to learn how to use it to our advantage.

This begins by knowing where worry comes from and how it's kept us humans from extinction for hundreds of thousands of years. We're talking about a natural, human stress response that evolved to help our ancient, cave-dwelling ancestors stay alert for threats like predatory animals. How? Well, when the imaginary worry lever creaks into action, it prompts the brain to release a natural chemical into the body system, called adrenaline . . .

Snarling beasts and surges of adrenaline

If we came face to face with a sabre-toothed tiger, back in prehistoric times, chances are we'd gasp and jump (I'd probably cry and scream). Those snarling beasts viewed us as breakfast, after all. Our heart would beat faster at the thought, and our breathing might quicken.

This physical reaction is down to a surge of adrenaline in the bloodstream. Adrenaline is a chemical messenger, also known as a hormone, which alerts the body to the fact that we might need to take emergency steps at any moment to avoid becoming the tiger's next meal.

Adrenaline increases our heart rate, which gets blood pumping to the muscles. It also prepares our lungs so we can process more air. In short, it quickly sets us up to take action. With a sabre-toothed tiger in our path, we'd have two options if we didn't want to become a meal. We could stand our ground and battle for survival (depending on our skills with a wooden club), or turn and flee for our lives. Whatever we choose, adrenaline is responsible for firing us up to get physical. This is known as the *fight or flight* response. It's designed to keep us out of trouble. Quite handy, eh? See, I did say our minds are pretty smart!

Today, unless we're *really* unlucky, we don't have to live in fear of attack by any kind of ferocious beast. Thankfully, sabre-toothed tigers are a threat from the past. (Our pet cats are a distant relation, but they don't tend to strike terror in our hearts!) But we're still equipped with the ability to experience

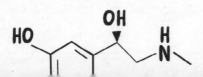

an adrenaline rush in the face of stressful situations. After all, life still presents us with lots of reasons to worry. We all have our own concerns, of course, from personal issues like body image or exams to wider topics that affect us all like the climate emergency.

Even if some worries are minor (like forgetting to do homework!) compared to the danger of being attacked by a hungry beast, if they trigger the release of adrenaline into our system, they can feel like a BIG deal. As a result, our mind and body go into a state of high alert. This can cause problems if there's no reason to run away and nothing to face and fight. Instead, all that adrenaline surging through our bodies leaves us all fired up or even stressed and anxious, and this can put a strain on our mental health.

So while a little worry might be a good thing, it can become a problem if we find ourselves fretting about one thing after another. Even a series of low-level worries can produce the stress response that releases adrenaline. This means we can exist in a state of constant alert for a threat that doesn't really exist. This is known as anxiety.

A worrier's guide to anxiety

Anxiety is a term that is often used to describe feeling worried for long periods of time – sometimes about different things – and often with no obvious cause. In this state of mind, your subconscious brain can conjure up reasons to explain why your body system is sloshing with adrenaline. Even if there's no cause for concern in your life, it'll find something for you to fret about to justify why you're feeling so restless, tense and unsettled.

What is a panic attack?

☆ In some cases, anxiety can lead to panic attacks. This is an extreme response and it can be frightening to experience.

☆ Sufferers feel an overwhelming sense of helplessness, while physical symptoms from the rush of adrenaline can range from a rapid heart rate to hyperventilation (rapid breathing) to sweating and feeling sick. This can even reinforce the sense that bad things are happening, leaving the sufferer feeling gripped by dread or panic. For example, some people who experience the symptoms of a panic attack mistakenly believe they are seriously ill or even dying. Working as an Accident and Emergency doctor, I've seen anxiety sufferers come in thinking they are physically ill. They can often be in great distress.

☆ Some people are unaware that they're feeling anxious, and the attack can take them by surprise.

☆ If you find yourself in the grip of a panic attack, try to remember that it's a physical response to mental distress. It's caused by anxiety flooding your system with adrenaline – but that unpleasant feeling *will* pass. If possible, let someone know what you're going through. It can help you to recognise that this attack is caused by an anxious mind rather than an actual threat.

☆ Controlling your breathing is key. Try the breathing exercise on the next page and aim to keep it smooth and steady until the symptoms of the panic attack pass.

Breathing Exercise

Some people find that breathing exercises help to ease the symptoms of anxiety. This is because when you breathe deeply, it increases your oxygen levels and sends a message to your brain that tells it to relax. Breathing exercises don't take very long and, even better, they can be done anywhere. Here is one you can try:

1. With relaxed shoulders and your head upright, breathe in slowly and deeply through the nose.
2. Feel your lungs filling with air, then breathe out slowly through the mouth.
3. Purse your lips to be sure the air leaves nice and gently.
4. Repeat the process for a minute, or until you feel a sense of calm return.

Living with anxiety can be draining. If we're constantly primed to *fight or flight*, it's hard to relax, recharge and even sleep. Many of us have been in that situation where we want to kick back on the sofa but we're too busy fretting about whatever's on our mind. It clouds everything. Even if we're tired, it can leave us feeling twitchy and stressed. The trouble is, when we're worn down by anxiety it's easy to lose sight of the fact that it can be overcome. It can begin to feel like a way of life, which is why it's so important for us to check in with our feelings on a regular basis. In every case, help is always out there to get things back on track – by either taking steps ourselves (check out my favourite mindfulness exercises on page 193) or talking to someone we trust who can help.

When I look back at my worry years at school, I realise now that anxiety played a part in leading me to believe my teachers secretly hated me. There was no evidence to support this, but my brain needed something to make sense of why my adrenalised system was in such a state of high alert. For a while, my brain did a weird kind of maths. It would take **anxiety** and add **overthinking**, and the result would be **a very worried Alex** who was convinced he could do nothing right.

As soon as I began to understand the causes of anxiety and act constructively whenever I worried, life calmed down a lot. I still worry to this day. Every now and then my mind will have a moment that sends me into a state of high alert. The difference now is that I know how to handle it and even use it as motivation to get stuff done.

Heads up

Here is my handy guide for bringing worry under control:

 A worry is a way for the mind to tell us that we need to take action. It's asking us to stand and fight or take flight. The only way to manage worry is to work out what is triggering it and identify the root cause of your concerns, so that one worry doesn't simply lead to another.

 Hiding from a worry doesn't make it go away. I know sometimes worries seem scary and leave us wishing we could live under the bedsheets or even move to the moon. The trouble is that worry won't just go away. If anything, it'll start to feel like a bigger and bigger problem. In every case, the best way to deal with a worry is by facing it. It takes courage, but there is always a way forward.

 Unleash the Lifelines: Writing our worries down in a journal or on our phones, or telling someone we trust, can help us get a grip on what's troubling us. Sharing a worry in this way can also help us to make sense of what's behind it and remind us that we're not alone in trying to make sense of our thoughts.

Set up an action plan. Setting up a plan can also help us create a sense of progress as we follow the steps we've set for ourselves. Let's say we've accidentally left our phone on the bus. (I know this is the second bus example I've used, but bear with me). Naturally, we're worried we'll never get it back. OK, so we could brood about it for ages, or we could put the problem into words and set up an action plan for getting it back! In this case, finding a quiet moment to tell a parent or carer will help us to feel less alone and own up to what has happened. If they can see that we're facing up to it with maturity, they'll want to help rather than give us a hard time. Together, the next step is to contact the bus company. We might have to wait for a while until the bus has returned to the depot, but if we receive news that the phone has been found, it means that worry disappears in an instant. Whatever the outcome, putting that plan into action has to be better than doing nothing then fretting and lying awake at night feeling like the world might just come to an end.

What's the worst that can happen? We touched on this before, but trying to imagine the worst thing that could possibly happen can often make our worries much easier to handle. OK, so we rang the bus company and they haven't got the phone. The worst thing that can happen is that we'll need to save up for another one and, in the meantime, we can use our friend's or parent's phone. And maybe, just maybe, we'll even enjoy a bit of time away from our screen. The worst thing that could happen isn't only manageable, it might even have some hidden blessings too!

There's only so much we can control. We all want to be in control of our lives but sometimes it's helpful to accept that we can't completely control *everything*. For example, we can't control that the family car broke down and made us late for school, we can't control that our sister was ill and so we missed that party we really wanted to go to, and we definitely can't control big things like war or poverty. But what we can control is how we adapt, act and respond to those things. It was the same when I was worried about letting people down or that people might be judging me. I needed to remember that people's thoughts and feelings are often beyond my control. But what I can control is how I look after myself, care for my mental health and turn my worries into positive opportunities.

Enjoy quality time. It's important to take a break from our worries if they're taking a while to sort through (alone or with someone who can help). Exercise is so useful here, whether it's a sport or just time out in fresh air. Even just having fun with friends can help us to feel brighter. We also have to make sure we're eating properly and getting enough sleep. If we're feeling refreshed – mentally and physically – we'll be in a better place to tackle whatever's on our mind.

Phobias

Sometimes people can develop an extreme fear of something, which is known as a phobia and can trigger a panic response.

People can develop phobias about all sorts of things, from animals to objects, places, food or even feelings. Even if there's no threat, sufferers experience a fear response that causes extreme anxiety and can even be strong enough to kick-start a panic attack.

Treatment is available for people with phobias – it involves slowly getting used to the cause of their fear until they recognise there is no threat.

YOU ARE **NOT** A
FAILURE FOR HAVING
BAD DAYS. YOU ARE
NOT A BURDEN FOR
HAVING BAD DAYS. YOU
ARE **NOT** A BAD
PERSON FOR HAVING
BAD DAYS.

CHAPTER 4

SORTING OUT STRESS

Next stop on our grand tour of the mind is stress. We often hear people talk about feeling 'stressed' or 'stressed out', but exactly what is going on here? Well, it's a natural response to feeling under pressure. We can be faced with it when we have too much happening in our lives, or when there is just something on our mind that is getting in the way of daily life.

Stress can often develop if we're leading busy lives. What with school, homework, sports and club activities, as well as time with friends and family, it can be hard to think of a moment in the day when we're literally doing nothing. We might not realise it, but squeezing so much into each day can make us feel emotionally tired. It can seem like we don't have enough time to do everything properly, which is a way of describing how it feels to be stressed.

Even though it can be a tiring experience, stress often makes it hard for us to unwind and even sleep well at night. This means that stress can become an exhausting experience.

Like worry and anxiety, stress can trigger the release of adrenaline into the body system. This can leave us feeling tense and on edge, and it's often associated with headaches. But stress is also one of those imaginary levers in our mind that we can pull to our advantage. Let's start by recognising what role stress plays in our lives. Our minds aren't deliberately setting out to make us feel overwhelmed and frazzled.

Phew!

Instead, it's a way of alerting us to the fact that we're under pressure and need to act. On my first day as a hospital doctor, working in the Accident and Emergency department, I felt nothing but stress. All of a sudden I was responsible for patching up patients, and that made my heart race. I had to remind myself that after years at medical school, I'd earned the right to wear my white coat. Even so, it took a while for me to get used to the responsibilities. Now, it's become a fast-moving job that I love! When handled positively, I really believe stress can motivate us to take on new challenges and make important decisions.

Heads up

Here's how to transform a difficult feeling into a force for action:

Identify the cause. When we're stressed, our mind is trying to tell us that we've got a lot to get through. So let's respond again by writing it all down and thinking about what is really making us feel frazzled. It's an effective way to visualise the cause and also find a moment of calm so we can consider our next step.

Work out what needs to be done. Come home from school with what feels like too much homework? Let's act on that stress by setting up a timetable to get through it. Set up a plan of action and stick to it.

Manage your time. We know that overcoming stressful situations often means working hard to get through it, but it's important to be kind to ourselves and build in plenty of rewards and rest periods. Not only does it feel nice writing 'biscuit break' between 'homework #1' and 'homework #2', it'll help you to keep everything under control.

77

Some people even use the Pomodoro Technique, where they break up their work into 25-minute segments with breaks in between. This was developed by an Italian called Francesco Cirillo and each break is known as a pomodoro. (Which is Italian for tomato! This isn't *completely* random. Francesco was inspired by the tomato-shaped timer he had in his kitchen at university.) The idea is that we work for 25 minutes, have a five-minute break and after three pomodoros, make our next break even longer. It can help with focus and time management, while also giving you those all-important biscuit breaks.

One step at a time. Often people feel like they can't cope when there's so much to be done. Try taking one step at a time when working towards a goal, rather than viewing the whole stressful situation and feeling overwhelmed.

Launch a Lifeline. Check in with a friend, or someone you trust with a listening ear, to help put the stressful situation into perspective.

Go easy. Dealing with stress can be tiring. If we push ourselves too hard, a stressful situation can seem even harder to overcome. People often talk about 'de-stressing', which is effectively any activity that helps us to relax, unwind and take our mind off the matter. Quality time with friends or family can work wonders, as can time to ourselves doing something we enjoy. This can be a different thing for each person. Me? If I'm in the middle of a tough day, I'll take myself away for fifteen minutes and go for a 'stomp'! This is what I call my short walk when I have something on my mind. The fresh air and change of scene always help me to work out what needs to be done when I get back. Give it a go!

My trusty stomp kit essentials

1. A bottle of water – hydration is key
2. Headphones for listening to music (classical music is very calming but I do also love a bit of Taylor Swift)
3. A pair of comfy trainers (there's nothing worse than getting blisters)

   . . . and if it's cold, don't forget to take a coat.

WHEN THINGS ARE HARD, TAKE IT DAY BY DAY. IF THAT'S TOO MUCH, TAKE IT HOUR BY HOUR. AND IF THAT'S TOO MUCH, TAKE IT MINUTE BY MINUTE.

Testing ... testing ... (managing revision, assessment and exam stress)

Homework, assessment and exams are something we all face at some stage and they can be a classic source of stress. For many, it's their first real taste of how it feels. Assessments and exams are designed to test us and see how we perform under pressure, so it is only normal that they're a little anxiety inducing. Sometimes I honestly wish exams had never been invented, but part of my self-help strategy is to remind myself that if I do the work, then it's also an opportunity to shine. And if I'm going to deliver to the best of my abilities, then I need to manage and face up to the challenging feelings that come as part of the package. This is how I try to do it:

☆ **Be prepared.** It can be tempting to put off preparing for assessments or revising for exams. I've lost count of the number of times I was supposed to have my nose in a medical book but instead found myself doodling pictures of silly dogs. The trouble is these tests won't go away. If we constantly put off preparing for them, our stress levels will just rise. Procrastination cycles can be tricky to break, but I promise it can be done (dog doodles included).

☆ **Make a revision plan.** Divide up your work in the time you have available so you can cover everything comfortably. Build in short breaks (remember our friend Francesco Cirillo!) and create quality time out as a reward for all your hard work. Stress level zero isn't *really* achievable, as a little stress is still a normal part of the revision experience, but it can be managed by sticking to the plan.

☆ **Protect your study space.** Aim to find somewhere quiet where you can revise undisturbed. This isn't always practical or easy at home. Families can be noisy, and very distracting. A zen workspace to calmly practise some maths problems can be easily destroyed by bickering siblings. If so, make full use of your school or local library. Any environment that allows you to focus will help to keep your stress under control.

☆ **Prepare to shine.** If we've done the work then we've also earned the right to go into that test or exam feeling ready to do our very best. A positive attitude, backed up by solid revision, can work wonders.

☆ **Lean on a Lifeline.** It's easy to get caught up in preparing for a test or an exam. That's why our Lifelines can be useful. I find it especially helpful opening up to a friend about how I'm feeling and doing something nice with them. Maybe you could do this as a reward after a study session together. We want to do well in our studies, of course, but it's good to do other things that remind us that there's more to life than just exams.

LIFELINES

☆ **Remind yourself of the goal.** Assessments and exams are a stressful business but believe it or not, life goes on once they're over. Although it might feel like it at the time, no missed homework, failed assessment or exam signals the end of the world. No matter what your results, you'll always have options. There have been times when I didn't get the results I needed. It's disappointing, but rather than thinking I was a failure and falling into despair, I realised I still had options – and that included retakes! The important thing is that we can look back knowing we did our best.

WHATEVER'S ON YOUR MIND, SHARING IT WITH SOMEONE YOU TRUST WILL ALWAYS LIGHTEN THE LOAD.

CHAPTER 5

BEATING THE BLUES

So, we've aced anxiety and sorted stress, but what about beating the blues? Next on our journey is sadness. It is easy for us to think of sadness as a negative, unwanted emotion. Everyone likes to be happy, after all. But even if sadness isn't something we welcome into our lives, it's a feeling that can help us to process moments in life that range from upset and disappointment to rejection, heartbreak and despair. While sadness can be difficult to experience, I'd like us to start seeing it as a stepping stone to better days. How?

Well, sadness can be described as feeling low in mood. Some people talk about being unhappy, which can mean the same thing. Sadness is often expressed through body language. Someone who feels sad might seem distant, as if they have something on their mind. In some ways, it's a signal to others that they need comforting or just time and space to work through their feelings. Sadness is a temporary emotion. Even if it feels hard to handle, it's important to remember this emotion will definitely pass and better days will come.

Shining a light on depression

Sadness can be a response to a difficult event, like falling out with a friend or not being picked for a team. But in some cases, it can set in for no apparent reason and without any sense that the situation will improve. The truth is that most people will go through periods of time where they feel sad or down, but if you feel persistently this way for weeks or months, it could be a sign of a mental health issue that can affect people in different ways. It's called depression, which is an illness that can be treated. If these feelings last for more than a few weeks, it's vital to ask for help from a health professional.

Depression affects one in four people at some stage in their lives. In particular, young people are often thought to be most vulnerable. Sufferers often feel hopelessly sad or even worthless. Some just feel numb and detached. Other symptoms may include feeling tired, sleeping problems, irritability and weight changes.

People can experience depression for all sorts of different reasons. It can be linked to events in life such as loss, stress, bullying, friendship and relationship difficulties, or linked to health issues such as hormone imbalance, changes in brain chemistry or blood sugar levels. Depression can last between three months and two years, but most cases are successfully treated, often through a combination of medication plus some form of talking therapy.

In my role as a doctor, I have seen how effective treatment programmes can be. The key to unlocking it is finding the courage to ask for help. That might begin by talking to a parent, teacher or doctor who can work with you to seek the help you deserve.

It's hard to know when feelings of sadness are a sign of a mental health illness like depression. Sometimes it can begin as a response to an upsetting event and then become a feeling that just sets in over our lives. But in every case, whether it's a sadness that will pass or something deeper, we don't have to deal with it alone.

Heads up

Here's how to find help if you're experiencing feelings of sadness:

 Reach for a Lifeline. We've said this before, but it really is so important. If you're feeling down and it's affecting your daily life, then don't be afraid to open up about it. Even if we're unsure if it's sadness or depression, sharing what's on our mind can only help us recognise that we don't have to go through this alone. Turning to friends and family who understand what's going on is a good first step towards recovery. Some people prefer to talk to a teacher or school counsellor. You can even call a helpline (see the Help Yourself section on page 215) and speak in confidence about your situation. It might take courage, but people will want to help.

 Get support from a doctor. As a Lifeline, a GP can make a professional medical diagnosis, and can also draw on a range of effective therapies. This might mean medication is an appropriate option as part of a wider treatment plan that can include counselling. A doctor will always answer any questions about all options available. They'll also review how treatment is going on a regular basis to be sure it's the best course of action at that time. Should we feel down for no clear reason, and the feeling lasts beyond a few weeks, we owe it to ourselves to make an appointment and talk things through. They'll want to help, and that begins by asking.

 Take care. As well as checking in with our doctor, it's important we're kind to ourselves too. Activities that help us to relax can help to beat the stress and anxiety often linked to depression. Exercise like swimming, jogging or football, or even just getting some fresh air

in nature, can make us feel more positive. Just don't rely on it as the only form of treatment. By considering all our options in tackling depression, we are better equipped to manage and overcome it.

A note about self-harm

(**Warning:** what follows might be upsetting for some readers and is best read with an adult.)

Sometimes people express strong or troubling feelings by hurting or injuring themselves. We can think of it as a physical expression of emotional pain. Self-harm can be triggered by lots of different causes, from depression and anxiety to traumatic or stressful episodes in life. Even though it can draw sufferers to cut, scratch or bruise themselves, the causes of self-harm go deeper than body image.

If self-harm is a concern, check out the Help Yourself section on page 215. Support is out there to help address the causes and find safer, constructive ways to deal with the feelings behind it.

When times are dark and the storm is hanging over our heads, it can be hard to see any chance of good times coming. But remember that the night is darkest before the dawn. Good times do come. Whoever you are, whatever you are battling, the storm will pass. Don't give up, speak to your loved ones, ask for help.

NO STORM HAS **EVER** LASTED FOR EVER.

CHAPTER 6

LONELINESS
UNLOCKED

Some people are happy in their own company. Others prefer to surround themselves with family and friends. Most of us enjoy a combination of the two, depending on where we are and what we're doing. Time alone can help us to focus on work or relax and recharge, while being sociable can help us to feel connected. There are times when I love being with friends, and also moments when I want to chill out by myself or sing out loud with my headphones on when there's nobody around to laugh. My dog might look at me strangely, but that's fine! It means that after I've taken him for a walk, I feel refreshed by my time out and ready to catch up with the world once more.

TAKE TIME TO BE FRIENDS WITH YOURSELF TOO. IT MEANS YOU'RE NEVER ALONE.

Human interaction is an essential part of life. Whether it's spending time with your family or having fun with your friends, human connection is one of the things that makes life so fun and meaningful. So if we feel it's something that's not easily available to us, a sense of loneliness can take shape in our minds. A bit like the worry warning system we talked about earlier, feelings of loneliness alert us, reminding us that we need to connect with others.

People experience feelings of loneliness in different ways and for different reasons. We might feel cut off from others, like friends and family, or be very sociable and yet still feel isolated and misunderstood.

Loneliness is often linked to how we feel about ourselves. If we don't feel confident and positive, or even understood, it can be hard to connect with others. As a result, loneliness is often an issue for people who live with other mental health conditions like anxiety or depression.

So, what is social anxiety?

Meeting new people or making friends isn't always easy. You might remember what it was like on your first day of school – it takes time to build trust and feel comfortable with each other. Often, we have to step out of our comfort zone to connect.

When I appeared on the TV show *Love Island*, I joined a group of people around my age to share a holiday villa for a few weeks. Everything was filmed for the show and would be viewed by an audience of millions! Naturally, I was nervous, but I just had to remind myself that everyone else was feeling the same way. Rather than hiding in a corner, I introduced myself to my new villa mates. Yes, it was awkward, but that's totally normal. We all went through the same experience. What's more, that feeling soon faded as we got to know each other, and it felt like we'd been friends for ages. If I can do that on

telly, you can definitely go say hello to that classmate you've always wanted to talk to.

Sadly, some people find it hard to overcome that nervous feeling when we meet new people or find ourselves in social situations. It can tap into anxieties that stop them from wanting to join in, being social and living their lives to the full.

But social anxiety shouldn't be confused with being shy. Many of us – including me – hold back a little in new situations until we feel relaxed and confident. This is totally normal, but for some it can be such a frightening prospect that they avoid them completely. We're not just talking about meeting new people face to face. Some individuals with social anxiety find it hard to speak on the phone or just be themselves in public, which restricts their daily lives.

Social anxiety is treatable. A doctor can make a professional diagnosis and talk through the options available, such as therapy.

We can help ourselves by taking small steps to address the issue. If the thought of joining a big gathering at the weekend is too much, consider spending time with a trusted friend instead. Slowly building our confidence can help us work towards expanding our social world. Just remember to take it one step at a time.

Heads Up

Loneliness can be overcome, whether we're feeling mentally or physically isolated. Here are some tips for reconnecting with the world around us:

Grab a Lifeline and identify the problem. If we're comfortable in most social situations but feel misunderstood or lacking in a sense of connection, it can be helpful to be honest with ourselves and talk it through with someone we trust. This might help identify the underlying problem. Plus, reaching out shows us that nobody has to live with loneliness. People care. They want to help. We just have to find the courage to ask.

Deal with underlying issues. Low self-esteem (not feeling good about ourselves) or depression can leave us feeling cut off even if we're a busy or outgoing type, but these are also mental health issues that can be addressed with help and support.

 A positive mindset. If the sense of loneliness comes from a lack of social contact, we can often feel trapped. A change of mindset can create opportunities to get in touch with friends again or even meet new people. It's good to start by thinking about the connections we have already. Are there people we already know that we could make friends with? Or is there someone in our lives that we trust and is always there for us, who we could spend more time with? Remember, we all have the power to make positive changes to our lives.

 Small steps. Taking ownership of loneliness can be daunting. It takes courage to reach out, but those who make the effort won't look back. The key is not to look too far ahead. Instead of thinking about becoming best mates with everyone overnight, focus on one or two people who have things in common with us. It doesn't have to be much. Maybe we've just streamed the same TV show recently or listened to similar music. By showing an interest, we can begin to build a bond.

Shared interests. Joining an after-school club or sports activity can help us meet new people. And if nothing appeals, why not start your own group or club and invite like-minded people to join? It's another opportunity to break free from loneliness. It might take a little effort, but our confidence can only grow along with our social circle.

Watch out for others. People can feel lonely for all sorts of reasons. If someone is new at school, for example, it can be overwhelming, or maybe a classmate is just finding it hard to fit in. Whatever the case, a kind word or invitation to hang out could mean the world to them. It might even earn you a new friend.

TALK TO YOURSELF LIKE YOU WOULD TALK TO A FRIEND, AND KNOW THAT HELP IS ALWAYS OUT THERE NO MATTER HOW ALONE YOU FEEL.

CHAPTER 7

LEARNING TO OVERCOME LOSS

We know that life is a roller coaster of ups and downs. While everyone loves the ups (also known as happy, fun and joyful times), it's important that we learn to survive the downs and be stronger for the experience. When it comes to getting through challenging moments, sadness can play an important role. It's normal to feel down when faced with disappointment or rejection, like when the club we support loses an important cup final or when we're not picked for a school team. The process helps us to move on.

But when someone or something important to us leaves our lives, the sense of loss can be devastating. We could be talking about anything from the break-up of a close friendship or romance, which means limiting our time around that person as we come to terms with our feelings, to the news that someone close to us has died.

We're talking about powerful feelings of sadness and upset that make it hard to imagine what the future will be like without them. We've lost an emotional connection, after all, and this can leave us feeling vulnerable – which means we feel exposed to upsetting feelings that might seem impossible to handle. Unfortunately the feeling of loss isn't something we can guard ourselves against. It's something we will all face at some point in life, but we can also overcome such painful moments. It doesn't mean we forget what's happened. It's just that loss becomes a part of our experience in life.

Bereavement

Dealing with the death of a loved one is sometimes known as grief or bereavement. It's a challenging emotional process. Experiencing a bereavement, and grieving for that loss, can often mean we spend long periods of time thinking about what's happened. There might also be other times when you feel more able to focus on life right now and enjoying the things you enjoyed before. And you might even find yourself fluctuating between these two stages – where you go through periods of reflection and pain, and then periods of moving forward or looking towards the future. This is OK and there isn't just one way to experience grief.

When it comes to dealing with any kind of loss, we can feel vulnerable and emotionally fragile, and even find it overshadowing everything else going on in our lives. It takes time to make sense of the situation. It's important to surround ourselves with people who know what's happened and have our best interests at heart. Talking to them can help process our feelings, but also let them help remind us that we will get through this feeling stronger for the experience.

Even though it's difficult, if we can view grief and bereavement as an important and necessary part of life that will affect us all at some stage, then it can become easier to manage. Eventually, we learn to live with the loss, and although we don't 'get over it', our lives can grow around it. It's about accepting what's happened and knowing those raw and painful feelings will get easier with time.

Understanding grief and bereavement

When my brother Llŷr died suddenly, it felt like my world stopped turning. He took his own life, which came as such a shock. I struggled to accept that he'd gone and found myself thinking about him constantly.

Emotionally it was the most painful experience I'd ever been through. It's not something you ever 'get over', but I can tell you that time is a great healer.

I learned to turn to friends and family and talk about difficult feelings. It wasn't easy, but I knew that just putting on a brave face was not the answer. Whatever challenges come our way, it's vital that we're able to open up about our emotions. I cried. I talked. I even laughed at memories of funny moments from Llŷr's life. I've learned to be open and honest about how I feel, which is the surest way to begin making sense of the loss of someone so important to me.

I still miss Llŷr terribly, but by dealing with the pain that comes with grief and bereavement I am learning to live my life without him, and this book is my way of honouring his memory.

At some stage, all of us will lose someone we cherish. Even the death of a pet can be hard to handle, especially if we feel that nobody will understand the emotional pain we're going through. In every case, grief can be managed. It's not something we can hurry or cure, but with support from those who care for us, we can find our own way through it, while treasuring the memories of those we have lost.

Often, it can feel like the emotions linked to grief come in waves. Sometimes those waves can feel strong and other times they're just ripples. Things will calm eventually, and while we all experience grief differently, it's worth recognising the emotions we can face along the way.

☆ **Shock and denial.** Whether the loss was expected or it takes us by surprise, it's common to feel quite numb to begin with. We can think of it as a way for the mind to protect us from distress and prepare us for the emotional pain ahead. Some people even find it so hard to process that they refuse to accept that it's happened.

☆ **Anger.** This might seem like a strange response, but often the death of someone important to us can seem

very unfair. Our emotions often run hot at this time, and it's normal for anger to feature as part of the grieving process.

⭐ **Sadness and longing.** This is perhaps the emotional response that everyone thinks of when it comes to dealing with loss. We can feel very down and fragile. Crying can be common and often catches us by surprise. We might also find ourselves thinking about our loss and wishing we'd used our time together differently. It's important to remember there is no wrong way to feel. We just have to give ourselves time and space to process the loss and go easy on ourselves while we do it.

⭐ **Acceptance.** No matter how we deal with grief, there will come a time when we can look back at what's happened and accept it. Sometimes it can seem like we've reached that point only to experience a setback of some sort. It could be a memory that catches us off guard and triggers strong emotions, or just a low phase after having felt like we were getting our lives back on track. This is totally normal. We'll never forget what we've lost, but things will eventually begin to feel less heavy and hard.

While everyone follows their own pathway through grief, at every stage, opening up to someone we trust can help us to make sense of our feelings. It can even work as a kind of emotional pressure release. Check out the resources in the Help Yourself section on page 215 for sources of care and support.

Heads up

Just as we will all face loss in our lives, there are also times when people close to us experience a bereavement. Here's how we can help:

 Respect how they deal with it. There is no rulebook when it comes to dealing with loss. Aim to recognise that whatever emotions that person is going through are all part of their grieving process. Even if they don't show a strong response, it's simply their way of processing what's happened.

Recognise that emotions will change. Grief can give rise to all sorts of different feelings. It's an unstable time, and some people can switch from one emotion to the next.

 Be ready to listen. People in grief often want to talk. Don't judge them or try to steer the conversation. Just offer them the chance to express whatever's on their mind.

Get practical. Grief can be so overwhelming that sometimes people seem to stop functioning normally. It means basic tasks can sometimes go forgotten, like eating regularly. We can help here with gentle reminders, or even stepping in by preparing a snack or a meal. Be smart here and just take care of things that person may not have time to consider while they're processing the loss.

Seek support. Try not to take on full responsibility for someone who is grieving. It can feel overwhelming for everyone. That's why we need to be sure to reach out for support ourselves. In some ways, Lifelines are just as important to those

111

who are caring for others as they are for those in need. Even if we just need to talk through how we're feeling, people will recognise and respect the effort we're making to help another person going through a tough time. What matters is that we open up to someone we trust, from a family member to a teacher, a close friend or school welfare officer.

TO ANYONE WHO HAS LOST A LOVED ONE, LET'S GET THROUGH TODAY TOGETHER.

CHAPTER 8

LET'S MAKE THE MOST OF FAMILY AND FRIENDS

No family is perfect. It's easy to think other people are leading better lives, but we never really know what's going on inside other homes. Every family experiences tension, stresses and strains. We're talking about a relationship we don't choose to be in, after all, and yet we're living under the same roof! It's only natural that we won't always get along.

I was lucky enough to get along with my family. But still, there would often be times when I didn't see eye to eye with my parents, and my brothers and I could squabble like it was an Olympic event. While nobody enjoyed those clashes, I eventually realised how important they were in teaching me how to get along with other people. I learned that compromise could quickly help to restore peace, which had to be better than refusing to meet in the middle and insisting that I was right and everyone else was in the wrong! I also realised that staying calm during moments of tension was more productive than yelling, stamping and storming off.

Of course, all families are different. We're raised in different ways and face different situations, and that gives every one of us a unique pathway as we grow up. Many families work well as a unit, which helps provide a sense of support, love and belonging. But other families might find there are challenges that make this more difficult. Whatever the case, no family is perfect. Like our mental wellness, we should see family relationships as a constant work in progress. This means it isn't just about enjoying the good times but also handling the pressure points, like the fallouts and disagreements. From a screaming match with a sibling to slamming doors and yelling things we don't really mean at other family members, most

of us have been there and regretted it. Sometimes it's just easier to talk things through or give one another a bit of space until we've calmed down. Everyone has a unique relationship with their family, but one thing is for sure: it's a learning ground for life.

Sometimes families will also reshape after a parental separation or divorce. It's a big upheaval for all involved, but ultimately it's the only way for everyone to find happiness again. The Help Yourself section on page 215 includes some resources if this is something you and your family are currently navigating.

At any time, no matter what our family set-up, we also all have a right to feel safe. If this becomes an issue and you can't turn to anyone inside the home, talk to a responsible adult who has your best interests at heart, such as a teacher or school welfare officer. Check out the Help Yourself section at the back of this book for details of support services. There is plenty of help out there to provide us with the protection we all deserve.

What are friends for?

We're pretty stuck with our families, but we *can* choose our friends, which means we can surround ourselves with plenty of brilliant people who make us laugh and who we can confide in. I can't count the number of great days I've spent having fun with friends and making memories. But although some friendships are destined to last for life, others will come and go. In every case, what matters is that the people we decide to be friends with show us respect and kindness, and that we show the same to them.

Without respect for each other, problems can develop within friendships that lead to upset, insecurity and unhappiness. Anything from jealousy to insensitivity can take shape, and that can turn a friendship into a source of anxiety and misery. It may even result in bullying, which is when it's time to ask if that person can really be a true friend.

Then there's the pressure we can find ourselves under to fit in. It's natural to want to feel like part of a group, but sometimes it's tempting to join in with behaviour that makes us feel uncomfortable, simply because everyone else is doing it. We could be talking about anything from being mean about someone behind their back to antisocial behaviour that we wouldn't dream of doing at any other time. When we experience this feeling, which is sometimes called peer pressure, it can be hard for us to say 'no'. At the same time, I really believe that if we can find the courage to say that single word and just politely steer clear of any activity we don't want to be involved in, people can only rate the fact that we're able to stand up for ourselves and we can walk away with our heads held high.

In every case, if anyone we're spending time with makes us feel small, worried, intimidated or pressured in any way, it's important to take time out. These people aren't true friends, and while that can be hard to accept, it's important to remember their behaviour says more about them than us. Moving on can be tough, so we need to surround ourselves with people who genuinely care for our happiness.

As for good, healthy friendships, they are important for many reasons. From just hanging out together, to celebrating each other's birthdays, to swapping books or generally having a laugh, there are plenty of great benefits to having a good circle of friends. Plus, if we're experiencing problems in other areas of our lives, such as at home or in school, it can help to hang out with friends who know what we're going through. When I found myself the target of bullies at school, my mates could see that it was making me miserable. With their encouragement, I told a teacher what was going on and they put a stop to it. Of course, there are times when we just want to get away from life's hassles by hanging out with friends, and that's fine. Even if we choose not to talk about what's bothering us, that quality time together can be exactly the break we need from what's going on elsewhere.

TOGETHER WE **ARE** STRONGER.

Heads up

Family life can have a big impact on how we're feeling. In the same way, friendships are important to us, for having fun and also as a source of support and understanding. But both inside and outside the home, there will always be moments when we don't all get along. If we want our friendships and family relationships to truly shine, then we have to put some work into them. Here's how:

 Open up. Our friends and family are brilliant Lifelines. They are there for us. Opening up to them is a powerful tool when it comes to overcoming any problem or difficulty we may encounter.

 Be a listener. As well as sharing what's on our mind, be prepared to let others have their say and be there for them, in the way they are for you.

 Prepare to compromise. Friendships and family relationships thrive when we learn to be flexible. We're all individuals, and sometimes our approaches to life can differ. That doesn't always mean one person is right and the other is wrong. In fact, a difference of opinion on any subject can be healthy if treated with respect. It can even be a source of fun. When it comes to football, I'm a massive Swansea City fan, but incredibly not everyone supports what is clearly the best team in the world! Sharing our views, even if we can't agree, is how we learn to deal with new ideas and discover things about life beyond our own experience.

FAMILY CAN MEAN WHATEVER YOU MAKE IT. A CLOSE FRIENDSHIP CAN LAST A LIFETIME, AFTER ALL.

CHAPTER 9

ONE BODY, ONE LOVE

The way we see our bodies can often shape how we feel about ourselves. If we're not comfortable with our appearance it can affect our self-confidence and hold us back. But in truth, no two bodies are physically the same. We are all different shapes, builds and sizes!

Throw in everything, from our skin to the texture of our hair, and that sets each person even further apart from another. What's more, our bodies develop as we grow up. Sometimes it can feel like we're living inside a stranger, which is why it's so important to make friends with our appearance. But more than that, I believe we owe it to ourselves to learn to value our inner beauty. From our personalities and sense of humour, to our interests and beliefs, if we consider ourselves to be decent individuals at heart then this is where our self-confidence begins.

But finding self-confidence isn't always easy, because too often we find ourselves viewing other people in terms of looks alone and feeling like we don't compare. Growing up, everyone physically matures at different rates. At school, a couple of my classmates appeared to transform from boys to men in the space of a term, which made me feel left behind. It was just so awkward being around these man/boy giants, especially when it came to getting changed for PE lessons! It took me a while to remind myself that they were still the same people on the inside. Their bumfluff moustaches didn't make them better than me, and I had no need to be embarrassed about my baby face. Yes, it earned them attention (for better or worse!), but it was still their personalities that made a lasting impression.

It's easy to feel insecure about our appearance. Why? Because there's almost always some feature about ourselves that we don't consider to be our strongest. As soon as we focus on it, of course, it's all we see! But remember, we are our own worst critics, and everyone always wants what they haven't got. I really wish I had thick curly hair like one of my best friends, but I know for a fact he wishes he had straight blond hair like mine. I could spend my time obsessing over my straight hair and booking myself in for a perm, or I could accept that my hair is perfectly fine as it is. And above all, whether my hair is curly, straight or completely non-existent, it doesn't *really* matter. What is more important is that I'm content and happy.

And even if we don't completely LOVE every single part of our bodies, we can be body neutral, which means that we accept how we look and recognise that we are more than our bodies. This neutral mindset means we can focus our energies elsewhere.

If we can learn to relax about how we look and adopt a positive attitude to eating and exercise too, that's when our personality can truly shine. If you ever feel like you need some help to switch up your mindset, try remembering the following:

☆ Our physical appearance is often the first thing that other people notice about us, but it's our personality that makes a lasting impression.

☆ It's only when we make peace with our body image that we can relax and truly be ourselves. By learning to be grateful for what we have, we can then look outwards rather than inwards and make the most of our lives.

☆ The human body is literally amazing. It still boggles my mind that all the cells in our body came from the division of ONE cell to make a unique package for each of us. Rather than focusing negatively on how things look, let's remind ourselves that our body is doing completely miraculous things all the time – like how the gut behaves like a second brain with its own nervous system (this brings a totally new meaning to trusting your gut!), or how bones can repair themselves (very handy), or how the mouth produces 1–2 litres of saliva each day . . . OK, that last one is a bit gross but you get what I mean – our bodies can do tons of things. So let's look after them and keep them working in tip-top condition.

Affirmations Exercise

We might be used to hearing compliments or giving them to others, but we don't really say them to ourselves (for fear of getting a big head, maybe). But some scientific studies have shown that self-affirmations can help boost our confidence and be a tool to help shift our mindsets.

So if ever you're feeling down or lacking in self-confidence and in need of a pick-me-up, look in the mirror and repeat these lines three times:

YOU ARE WORTHY.

YOU ARE GOOD ENOUGH.

A healthy attitude to exercise

We live at a time when we can transform images of our appearance with the touch of a button. From filters to editing tools, it may seem like harmless fun to begin with, but as a result, social media is filled with millions of seemingly perfect portraits of both celebrities and everyday people. Unless we're aware that so many pictures have been touched up digitally to smooth a complexion or make someone appear slimmer, it's easy to feel like we can't compare – especially when there isn't a single imperfection in sight, which ultimately wreaks havoc with our minds and self-esteem.

This can create the temptation to exercise in order to achieve a certain look, rather than to be fit and healthy. The trouble is, it rarely brings happiness. Why? Because we're chasing a goal that isn't real. It's filtered and polished. What's more, if we're constantly failing to reach our goal, then all that working out combined with the sense of disappointment can affect our mental health. It can be a vicious cycle.

It's time to build a healthy relationship with exercise and our bodies, and not let it rule our lives. In some cases, people can find that working out becomes a compulsion to block or escape from a sense of unhappiness about ourselves. A few years ago I was on holiday with my friends and found myself feeling really body conscious. I don't normally walk around with my top off, but it was a boiling hot summer's day and, sitting by the pool, I noticed every guy seemed to have a six-pack. I felt really self-conscious, like I just wanted to shove my top back on and go inside. It took me a while to realise that what we look like on the outside is literally just skin deep.

It really is our personalities that make the biggest impact. I don't remember people because of the size of their biceps or their taut, rippling stomachs – instead I remember them for the good times that we share just chatting and having a laugh. Nowadays, I work out to keep fit, rather than to achieve a look, and I love it. In every case, feeling good about ourselves has to come from within. This is why it's so important to exercise as part of a healthy, fun and positive lifestyle.

This begins by doing something active we enjoy. From team sports to solo workouts, if it's fun then getting fit is a bonus on top of the good times. It can also boost our self-confidence and mental wellness. In many ways, exercise is really just a form of movement. This means we don't always have to pick

a sport to look after ourselves. I really enjoy being active in any way, whether it's walking around the block to clear my head (the 'stomp', as I call it), sessions in the gym or a game of tennis with a friend so we can chat at the same time. I like how it leaves me feeling chilled out and ready to take on new challenges. This is down to the release of natural feel-good chemicals called endorphins. We can't rely on them to feel positive, but we can build movement, activity or exercise into our routines and enjoy the benefit to our mental health that comes with taking care of our physical health.

Heads up

We can all improve our relationship with our bodies, and I can tell you it's a lifelong practice. But it all comes down to being kind to ourselves. So rather than standing in front of the

mirror frowning at our stomachs or the slope of our shoulders, let's focus on something to celebrate.

 Instead of focusing on the body, look beyond your appearance and ask questions about your internal self. What do you like most about yourself?

 This could be a talent, a subject a school that you're good at or a hobby. Maybe you like volunteering, or perhaps you're really good at making your friends and family laugh, or you boss it every time you play video games against your mates. It can be anything!

 The more we focus on the internal parts that make us who we are, the less we'll place value on how we look, and that's when we can truly shine!

CHAPTER 10

FOOD FOR LIFE

Eating is an essential part of life, and that's not just because of all those nutrients and minerals that keep us alive – although that's important too. Food can bring us SO much joy, from sharing a meal with family and friends, to drinking a mug of hot chocolate as a pick-me-up when we feel a little down.

I thank my lucky stars that I have taste buds and a sense of smell to enjoy all the flavours Italian food has to offer – I love it all, everything from pizza to pasta. But our relationship with food isn't just about whether we're a foodie or even which side of the 'pineapple on pizza' debate we sit on (the correct answer is . . . actually, I won't get into that).

Often there's a link between food and our feelings – for example, we may not feel like eating and can lose our appetite when we feel down or stressed. What's more, when we think about body image, which we touched on earlier, our relationship with food also affects our self-esteem and overall wellbeing. It's important to be aware that problems can kick in when it feels like food has taken over our thoughts and behaviour, clouding everything. This can be anything from obsessing over food to controlling what we eat, or using food to manage our emotions by under or over eating.

A note on eating disorders

Anorexia nervosa is an eating disorder in which sufferers restrict what they eat, which means they're not getting enough nutrients to stay healthy, while people with *bulimia nervosa* often make themselves sick after consuming food. Lastly, binge eating disorder (sometimes described as compulsive eating) is a disorder where sufferers feel unable to stop eating. Each of these eating disorders are mental health issues that often require professional help, understanding and support, but they can be overcome.

Let's be clear: food is a fuel that we should enjoy. There's a whole world of taste, texture and flavour out there, and a smart, balanced, healthy approach to eating can only benefit our physical health. Good food doesn't just help us make the most of life. It's something we can embrace as part of making each day count.

☆ A healthy, balanced diet is key to a positive mindset.

☆ This is the food we eat on a regular basis, and there's room in it for all sorts of different meals.

☆ A takeaway is totally fine every now and then, and often a fun way to enjoy time with family and friends. Just consider it to be a treat and not something to have every day.

☆ Our relationship with food is lifelong. So let's make it something positive and enjoyable, which benefits our mental wellbeing as much as our physical health.

A HEALTHY BALANCED DIET...

...HELPS A POSITIVE MIND

A note about diets

Thinking about food in terms of body weight can cause all sorts of difficulties for people. We're talking about dieting, which is a term used to describe cutting down or changing what we eat in the hope of losing weight. It can also be tempting to restrict what we eat as a means of controlling our appearance. At a time when I felt that having rippled stomach muscles was a passport to success – which it wasn't – I avoided certain foods I loved because I worried they would make me pack on the pounds. This isn't healthy for our bodies or our minds. It made me anxious and also hungry! Eventually, I realised that my happiness, an active life and good health were all that mattered. From there, I never looked back!

We know that simply dieting to lose weight doesn't work. It can increase stress and anxiety and even distort our relationship with food. Restricting what we eat can also mean that we miss out on nutrients and vitamins that fuel both our physical and mental health. What's more, people who diet often find they put the weight back on afterwards, which risks disappointment and unhappiness.

Only a doctor or qualified dietitian can advise someone to lose weight for health reasons, and this is done not just by changing their eating routine but in combination with an appropriate exercise programme. If your eating habits are ever a concern, you can check in with your GP at any time. They'll want to help, even if it's just to fine-tune your approach to physical and mental wellness.

YOU ARE BEAUTIFUL – INSIDE AND OUT.

CHAPTER 11

MAKING SENSE OF ME (THAT MEANS YOU)

What does it mean when we say we're one of a kind? We're all human, of course, but many different components go into making us unique.

Our identity can mean lots of things. Basically, it comes down to who we are and the things that make us ourselves. Try to imagine it like the ingredients of a cake or the layers of an onion. We might be into a certain type of music or sport, while all sorts of factors like our background or friendships play a role in making us individuals. As humans we are different from each other in many ways, and yet we also share common bonds. It means our identity can give us a sense of belonging with other people as well as the confidence to help us feel proud to be individuals.

The great thing about our identity is that it isn't fixed. It can change and grow over time. It's made up of lots of things, after all, including interests and beliefs, and these take shape in different ways. Sometimes we discover parts of our identity that stay with us for life, like my soft spot for puppies and summer holidays. Meanwhile, we might leave behind other things that no longer fit with how we see ourselves. This is good news. For me, it means I'm not destined to permanently wear those skinny jeans that I once thought looked cool even though I could barely walk in them. So let's not think of our identity as set in stone, but as something we can mould and shape at any time. In some ways it's how we keep growing as individuals throughout our lives.

Understanding our identity, getting comfortable with who we are and learning about who we want to be are things we all experience. As we grow up and start to think more about our identity, it's only natural that we reach for labels. It can help us to fit in with a group and feel like part of a tribe. Whether we get behind a football team or join a book club or TV show fandom, feeling like we belong can be a buzz. It's comforting in some ways and helps us to connect with like-minded people. The trouble is that often we don't fit neatly under a particular label. It can be confusing or leave us feeling uncomfortable if we're still working things out. It's important to remind ourselves that it's perfectly OK to have questions and not yet have worked out the answers.

While labels can be useful, it's important not to feel like we have to use them. It can certainly feel like we need to use a label if we're under pressure to fit in with a certain group, for example, or if we start noticing we have romantic feelings for someone and then question what that means.

Some of us might even feel unsure about our sexuality – which is a part of our identity concerned with who we are attracted to, whether it's boys, girls, both or none. And some people might question their gender identity. This is an expression that refers to what we feel like and whether we identify as a boy, girl or neither. It's different to our biological sex, which is defined by the body parts we were born with and whether we're biologically male or female – it's more about what we feel like inside. A small number of people feel that their biological sex does not match how they feel inside, which may mean they are transgender.

Some people get to grips with their sexuality and gender

without giving it much thought, while others need time and even a chance to express themselves in a certain way to see if it feels right for them, and that's fine.

In every case, each and every one of us is on our own journey. The decision to use labels is also personal. What matters is that we're content with who we are and comfortable with expressing ourselves, even if we're still putting together the pieces of the puzzle that reveals us to ourselves and to the world. It's not a race, and the most important thing is to remember those Lifelines, because help and support is always available. Whether we're after a casual chat or we're feeling troubled or distressed, putting feelings into words will help make sense of them.

Growing up, if I tripped over and grazed my knee, I was encouraged to 'be brave' and 'man up' about it. That meant it wasn't cool to cry. Boys didn't do that kind of thing – or so I was led to believe. It was only as I got older and started to question what it meant to carry the label of 'boy' or 'man' that I realised keeping a lid on my feelings in this way wasn't healthy. Emotions aren't divided up between boys and girls. Each and every one of us is free to express ourselves in any way that feels natural.

Heads up

We can all take a positive approach to our identities. In working out what makes us who we are, the key is to be comfortable with ourselves at all times.

There's no rush to get to grips with identity. Even if we're confused or unsure about some aspect of who we are, that doesn't mean we've fallen short or failed in any way. It just means we're still in the process of working things out.

Labels aren't compulsory. A label can help us to find our tribe, of course, but let's not forget that we are all still individuals! What makes us unique can be a source of pride, and if we stand out for being confident and kind, that's a great foundation for mental wellness.

Enjoy the journey. Coming to terms with what makes us tick can take time. It's more of a slow reveal than a sudden realisation, with lots of experiments like dodgy haircuts along the way. Once we recognise that we'll find out who we are in our own way, it can make life more enjoyable and be a source of growth when it comes to mental wellness, rather than a cause of uncertainty.

143

CHAPTER 12

MAKING RELATIONSHIPS ROCK

As we grow up, our feelings develop and strengthen. In general, we get to grips with our emotions by experiencing them, which is why we learn not to throw tantrums like we did as toddlers when things don't go our way. (No matter how strong the urge.) Even so, many other emotions can rise up inside us as we go through life and prove hard to handle.

Let's take feelings of attraction. When this emotion switches on, it can be intense. This is especially the case when we're new to the world of romance and relationships. We might find ourselves thinking about someone we really like and even daydreaming about them. It can be wonderful, of course, but there are times when falling for someone can feel more like an emotional challenge that's hard to overcome.

At my school, if a boy or girl fancied someone they'd often behave *really* strangely. Rather than getting to know them to see if they felt the same way, they'd act like it was the last person in the world they'd want to date! 'Eurgh, no way!' they'd claim when questioned if they liked them, even though deep down they couldn't stop thinking about that person. It was a weird way to express themselves, but then when I fell for someone for the first time, I found I couldn't even make eye contact with them! I realise now that we just weren't ready to handle feelings of attraction, which can take us all by surprise. In my case, instead of being open and honest, I made every attempt to cover up my emotions by pretending that the person I found deeply attractive didn't even exist! As a way of earning a date, I had a lot to learn . . .

Eventually, we all grow up and take responsibility for our feelings. We realise that if we want to get anywhere with someone we like, it definitely doesn't help to pretend that they're invisible or so repulsive they make us feel ill! Not only is it pointless but it's also disrespectful, and we can all be better than that.

It takes courage to open up about how we're feeling, but it's also a learning experience that helps us to make meaningful connections with people. Forming a bond with someone special can be hugely rewarding, but it takes time, effort and good communication skills. Often, we have to learn by our mistakes, and that can bring on a whole load of different emotions, from worry to upset to heartbreak.

All about crushes and first love

Love can be a powerful emotion. It's a mixture of admiration, respect, trust, attraction and even passion, and it's a feeling that often builds over time between two people in a relationship.

Sometimes we can find ourselves attracted to someone and think we're in love. In reality, that feeling has to be shared for it to thrive. Often, we can be attracted to someone we don't know in real life, such as a social media influencer or a movie star. This is called a crush. Feeling attracted to someone in this way can be an enjoyable experience. Think of it as an introduction to love and relationships. It's a safe way to get in touch with strong emotions. It also means we're familiar with that feeling of attraction for when we meet someone in real life who we really like, which can help us to relax as we get to know them and find out if they feel the same way.

Just be aware that for love to become a reality, we have to get to know that person and find out if they share the same feelings.

A crush can come and go. They're completely normal, and they're a fun, safe introduction to feelings linked to real-life romance. Problems only kick in for some people if they reach a point where they feel denied an actual relationship with that person. As a result, the crush becomes a source of pain and sadness. If this happens, confiding in someone we trust or writing in a journal will help us to work through our feelings, so that we can look to the future and find a realistic relationship with someone who shares our affections.

Even when we form a real relationship, there's no guarantee the attraction will turn to love. It might be something we read in books and see in films and on TV, but it doesn't have to be the ultimate goal. In reality, what matters when we get together with someone is that we share the same sense of respect and sensitivity for each other. This way, whether loves grows in the relationship or we find it doesn't last – or even if we ask someone out only to be rejected – we can look back knowing we handled it as best as we could.

Heads up

Being in a relationship doesn't make us more complete than someone who is single. It's easy to feel anxious when other people we know start dating, but we have to be comfortable with who we are before we can find happiness with someone special. There really is no rush to get into a romance at any time. Some people are happy making the most of their life without a boyfriend or girlfriend, and that's totally fine.

If and when the time comes that we do feel attracted to someone and ready to act on it, here's how to be constructive in managing both the ups and downs of a relationship:

Get to know that person first. People often worry about how to ask someone out. This can be stressful. Start by getting to know them and showing an interest in them as an individual. Just be a friend and see how they respond.

Relax with each other. The more time we spend with someone, the easier it is to be ourselves. This can often lead to a date or relationship.

Communication counts. In any relationship, we need to be open and honest with each other at all times. It's important that we share our feelings, hopes and any worries, and do so with respect. This means listening as much as talking, and it means learning to negotiate both fun and challenging times.

Consent. In any relationship, we all have the right to decide on what we do and do not want to do, and we can

also change our minds at any time. Just because you're in a relationship this doesn't mean you are obligated to do anything you feel uncomfortable with, or feel pressured to do, to please somebody else and vice versa. We should never assume that our partner is OK with doing anything either – for example, someone might not want to be kissed or asked personal questions, in person and online. Remember, communication and respect is key.

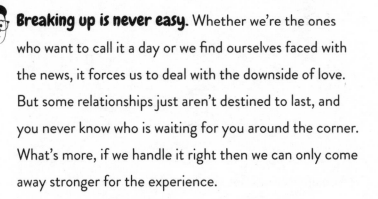

No shame. Not all relationships last for ever. They can just burn out, or one person may not feel able to return the same feelings. It's absolutely no cause for shame or embarrassment. Try to deal with it calmly, sensibly and sensitively.

Breaking up is never easy. Whether we're the ones who want to call it a day or we find ourselves faced with the news, it forces us to deal with the downside of love. But some relationships just aren't destined to last, and you never know who is waiting for you around the corner. What's more, if we handle it right then we can only come away stronger for the experience.

A Lifeline for love. The end of a relationship can give rise to raw emotions. Whatever we feel is OK and completely normal, even if the feelings seem unbearable. Don't bottle it up. Turn to a family member or friend and let them know what's happened. It will hurt for a while, but time will bring acceptance that it's over – and that can only set us up to handle future relationships better.

A note about toxic relationships

Sometimes we can find ourselves getting together with someone only to find they don't have our best interests at heart. They might have challenging issues of their own that they bring to the relationship, or they might not give us the respect that we all deserve. Complications can kick in if we have developed feelings for that person even when being with them doesn't make us feel good. We may even feel trapped or fearful of what might happen if we try to break up.

This is known as a toxic relationship. For people who find themselves in this situation, it can put a strain on their mental welfare and sometimes even put their physical safety at risk.

In every case, we all have the right to be both safe and happy. This can be found by reaching out for help. With support, from a family member or responsible adult, anyone in a toxic relationship can create an exit plan that puts their safety first and gives them every chance of moving on to find the happiness they deserve.

BE COMFORTABLE WITH YOURSELF AND YOUR PERSONALITY WILL SHINE THROUGH.

CHAPTER 13

CONNECTIONS THAT COUNT

Social media allows us to feel connected to the outside world, far beyond just the people we know in real life. The online world is a big community – apps like TikTok and Instagram have over a billion users. That's a lot of people. While it can feel like it's the place to be, most platforms need users to be a certain age before they're allowed to sign up, and this is to keep us safe from possible risks before we're ready. Once we are, for the sake of our mental wellness, as well as our personal safety, we need to treat social media with respect. This begins by recognising a platform's rules (and remembering that you have to be over thirteen to sign up for most platforms) and always informing a trusted adult before signing up.

After my time on television, I found myself in the virtual spotlight. Online, people talked about me, for better or worse, in ways that we might think twice about in a face-to-face situation. The online trolls were out in full force, saying all kinds of hurtful things. It made me feel like public property. The experience came as quite a shock, and I needed time to adjust in order to turn it into a positive force.

So, speaking as someone who has found themselves the focus of online attention, here's what we need to consider in order to make social media a healthy and rewarding part of our lives:

⭐ Social media gives us the potential to reach people we wouldn't otherwise meet in the real world.

⭐ When used with care and attention, and respect for others, it can actually be a useful tool for communicating and bringing out the best in us all.

⭐ But anything we share online could be used against us. Post or comment without thinking and we can invite a response that feels out of our control. We leave digital footprints when posting online, as anyone can look back through our social media history – which means one careless post or comment could come back to haunt us.

As well as considering our own responsibilities, we need to stay aware that any social media presence can make us a target of unwanted interest or even abuse. Not everyone we might meet or speak to online is who they seem, and they can have different intentions to what we think. Grooming can occur online too. This is when an adult builds a relationship with a young person so that they can manipulate, abuse or exploit them. Often these adults might use the same websites, games and apps as young people – they might create a fake online profile and pretend to be younger than they are. They might also employ various tactics such as offering gifts, giving a young person lots of attention to earn their trust. This is illegal and must be reported to a trusted adult immediately. The NSPCC and Childline have free helplines where anyone with concerns about grooming can call and talk to a counsellor anonymously (you can find out how to contact them in the Help Yourself section on page 215).

☆ We should never send our personal details to anyone, unless it is someone we trust, and we should never post personal information – like phone numbers or addresses – on any website, as this information could be found by anyone, especially if our profiles are public.

☆ Mute, Block and Report are all tools we can use to avoid seeing certain comments and to report posts that are of a serious nature. It might not be a perfect way of avoiding harm, but we have some control over what we see.

Ultimately, a life online is no substitute for the connections to be found in the real world. In many ways, it's not a reflection of reality. People have the ability to pick and choose what they share, after all. It might be helpful to think of it like a highlight reel – people don't often post a photo or a video when they're unhappy or going through a low moment. They can even edit photographs and videos with endless filters and apps to show themselves off in a good light. If we can remind ourselves of this when we use social media, we're less likely to look at our own lives and feel like we don't compare.

Let's talk about likes

Social media can sometimes feel like one big popularity contest. Our profiles showcase who we follow and who follows us, while the value of our posts is often measured by the number of likes and shares. This can make it easy to compare our profiles to others and feel like we're not as good as them. Some research has also shown that we can get addicted to the buzz of receiving likes, because each heart or thumbs up stimulates the reward centres of our brains. So when our posts are liked, it makes it even trickier to log off and to stop measuring ourselves against these likes.

EPIC

FAB!

LOVE

OMG

YESSS

COOL

@

@

When it comes to what posts and profiles prove to be popular, remember that clever computer code called *algorithms* make all the decisions. It might help the social media platform build an audience, but it can make many users feel sidelined or ignored.

In every case, the key is to remind yourself that online likes are no reflection of the connections we make in the real world, which is what really matters. We all know that it's more meaningful to count on one or two close friends than to be a familiar face to hundreds of strangers. I'd like us all to focus on the fact that our lives offline have a lot to offer. This way, our online time can be a valuable experience without us feeling like it's the only place to be.

NEVER BE JEALOUS OR ENVIOUS OF THE ILLUSIONS CREATED BY SOCIAL MEDIA.

Heads Up

Here's how to be smart about using social media, and how to use it as a force for good:

 Set boundaries. It's good to stay aware of how much time we're spending on social media, and cut back if it's getting too much. There's no substitute for quality time offline in the company of people who rate and respect us.

Think before typing. Sharing words and images can have consequences. The simplest way to make sure that we're making a positive contribution is by first asking ourselves whether we'd do the same thing in a face-to-face situation.

Be kind. This is the simplest way to be responsible in our relationship with social media. Quite simply, it means never posting anything offensive or cruel, or which might seem funny at someone else's expense. If we can stand by everything we share online, it can become a caring, creative and empowering space.

Caution is king. Some people feel safer and more comfortable making their profile private, so only family and friends they know can interact with them. Avoid taking risks online, like sharing personal information, and adopt a cautious attitude. If someone reaches out who you don't know, remember that they are strangers. We should never reveal information about ourselves that could compromise our safety in the real world. It's a small and simple precaution, but one that brings peace of mind online.

Address any issues. If your social media use is becoming a source of upset, anxiety or even misery, be sure to tell someone who has your best interests at heart. From finding yourself the target of online trolls (who set out to make you feel bad or humiliated) to receiving unwanted attention, every problem can be improved by reaching out for help.

Take a social media break. At any time, it's always worth stepping away and reconnecting with the offline world. It might seem unthinkable when we're scrolling through posts, but the reality is that time spent away from the screen is good for our mental health. Our profiles will still be there when we return feeling refreshed and refocused on making the online world a rewarding part of life.

Offline. Online. Lifeline. Social media can create both possibilities and problems, and it's vital that we stay connected to people we know and trust when reaching out for help. While there are great sources of support online, it's always good to tell an adult who's responsible for our welfare about any connection we might make and to put our safety first at all times.

> DON'T LIMIT YOURSELF TO A LIFE ONLINE. GET OUT THERE AND MAKE THE MOST OF THE REAL WORLD.

PART THREE

A BETTER DAY

CHAPTER 14

MENTAL STRENGTH AND OVERCOMING FAILURE

I didn't conquer my worries overnight. When I was at school, it took me a while to recognise that none of my teachers actually hated me at all. Once I realised that they wanted the very best for everyone, including me, I was able to build strategies to stop me fearing the worst. I had to learn to accept that if I did my best, whether in homework or exams, then the results would take care of themselves.

My experience isn't unique to me. We all face challenges with our mental health and often figure out how to address them in our own ways. We are each on a different journey. The good news is there are lots of exercises and activities we can embrace that help us to shine. What's more, they can be fully customised to suit ourselves and our lifestyle.

So this is the section of the book where we'll get to grips with how to help ourselves. Most importantly, I want it to be fun. Why? Because if we can enjoy taking care of our mental wellness then it quickly becomes a way of life. And if we can spread the word so others feel the benefits, that means we can all play a role in a major mental health movement too.

> **JUST BECAUSE SOMEONE IS DOING IT DIFFERENTLY TO YOU, DOESN'T MEAN YOU ARE DOING IT WRONG.**

Testing times (make us tougher!)

Every now and then, I still find that the confidence I built to deal with my anxieties can suffer a wobble. This happened to me in sixth form. After working hard on my A levels, I failed to get the grades I needed for medical school. Yes, it came as a shock and left me deeply disappointed. At first, it felt like the end of the world! I drifted around thinking all my chances in life had just gone down the drain, feeling like my lifelong dream of becoming a doctor was slipping away.

Then, with support from my parents and by talking to my teachers, I realised that my results still gave me options. So,

rather than despair, I set up a plan to retake my exams. It meant I had to retake a whole year at school. On the second attempt, after constantly reminding myself that I was doing the right thing, I passed! As a result, I went to medical school feeling mentally stronger because of the experience. I'd faced disappointment and learned good things from it. Nobody likes to be rejected, but by focusing on how I could improve I was able to face the future rather than dwelling on the past. I made the most of my retake year, not just by studying but by having fun with friends too, and that all helped me to achieve my dream and become a doctor.

Throughout our lives, our mental wellness faces many challenges. If we're going to tackle a setback, disappointment or difficult feeling, we need our minds to be in the best shape possible at all times. As we discussed in Part One, we take care of our bodies so we're in good physical condition. We should start doing the same thing with our headspace!

Nobody should feel like they *need* to have a problem with their mental health in order to make the most of the strategies I'm about to share either. We're simply talking about simple tweaks to the way we live that make our mental wellness a priority.

Life will always have its ups and downs. Just as we know how to enjoy the good times, we owe it to ourselves to be equipped to deal with difficult moments. It means that whatever the future holds for us, we can face it with a positive mindset. Using practical steps and simple exercises, I want us all to embrace mental wellness as a source of strength and springboard for success. Let's go! Or as I like to say, onwards!

Get resilient

If someone won an arm wrestle without even blinking, we'd think of them as physically strong. We might imagine them to be fit, and we would probably guess that they've spent a long time training and working out to get into that shape.

So, what do we mean when we say that someone is mentally strong? Firstly, we can be sure that it's not reflected by the shape and size of their body. We're talking about resilience here, which is a term used to describe someone's ability to deal with difficult or challenging times. The truth is, we all go through tough times, face big challenges and make lots of mistakes in the process. Trust me, I fail all the time. But it's OK, because failure helps us to learn, develop and grow. Take, for example, my favourite Formula 1 driver, Sir Lewis Hamilton, who throughout his teenage years flew off the track and crashed his go-kart countless times. He could have sacked it all in and given up. But he didn't. He learnt from each experience and eventually went on to be the greatest Formula 1 driver of all time (in my opinion!). This is mental resilience in action. So each time you fail, try to stop, reflect, pick yourself up and go again. If you can do this, you will be truly resilient.

☆ **Resilience is a quality we can all learn to embrace.** It's available to us all. No previous experience required, hooray!

☆ **It begins by changing the way we look at mistakes and setbacks.** We're talking about anything from a disappointing grade in a test, or even finding it difficult to grasp a new topic in class, to feeling sad because we didn't get picked for a sports team. Instead of giving up, turn the experience into a learning opportunity.

☆ **Look for ways to improve.** The resilient person will revise and retake the test, ask their teacher or friend to explain the topic again, or check in with their sports coach on what they need to work on to make it on to the team next time. Then they'll work on it to get there. Cue training montage with epic theme song!

☆ **Stay positive.** Even if things don't work out straight away, every attempt will help to build resilience. As an approach to life, it can only encourage confidence and help to set us up with a positive mindset no matter what obstacles we face.

> **DON'T BE AFRAID TO START OVER AGAIN. THIS TIME, YOU'RE NOT STARTING FROM SCRATCH. YOU'RE STARTING FROM EXPERIENCE.**

Recognise mistakes

Let's face it, none of us are perfect. If we look back on our lives, or even just the last few days, there's always something that we know we could've handled better.

At school, I took part in a debating competition. I was part of a team, which was a great honour. In the competition, each member took it in turns to go up against someone from another team and try to win a discussion using reason and public speaking skills. I enjoyed the challenge . . . I also liked to win. In this particular competition, however, I knew the opposition were strong. In fact, there was a good chance we would lose. So, rather than do my best, I pulled out. I just refused to take part, making the excuse that I was too busy, even though it meant I was letting my team down.

It was only afterwards, when I reflected on how I'd handled the situation, that I realised I had made a mistake. I'd put my desire to win before my teammates, and it left me feeling terrible. A day or so later, I apologised to them all, as well as to my teacher, and vowed never to make the same mistake again. Now, if I'm asked to do something with no guarantee of success, I'll work extra hard to do my best. Whatever the outcome, I know from experience that it's the right thing to do.

Sometimes our mistakes are minor. At other times, we might have allowed ourselves to fall into a pattern of behaviour where other people suffer as a result. Bullying is a good example of this, and if almost a third of young people report being victims, that means a great many others are somehow responsible. This might be an uncomfortable truth for some, but in many cases we might not even stop to think that our behaviour has left someone humiliated or upset. The fact is, most bullying isn't

down to people setting out to be bad on purpose. It's often down to being thoughtless, getting carried away with mates or putting our feelings before others, and if we just stopped to think about the consequences, I have no doubt that we would change.

So let's consider this moment to be a turning point. We all make mistakes, but it takes courage to admit to them and then turn what's happened into an opportunity for personal development. Here is some advice to get started:

☆ **Review behaviour.** We need to be honest with ourselves here. Have we ever joined in with a joke in which we laughed at someone else's expense, for example? It's easily done, but if we just pause to consider how embarrassed, awkward or even miserable that person felt as a result, we might have done things differently.

☆ **Take responsibility.** It's easy to make excuses and claim we only laughed because everyone else did, but it takes just one person to make a change for the better.

☆ **Lead by example.** We all have the ability to learn from our mistakes. It's down to each of us to make it happen. If we can improve, chances are that others will follow.

☆ **Enjoy peace of mind.** The great thing about learning from mistakes is that it feels good. We can take pride in the fact that we're willing to be better. It shows humility, honesty and a willingness to improve.

WHAT IF I
CAN'T DO THIS?
BUT WHAT
IF I CAN?

CHAPTER 15

GET MOVING AND CREATING

Get active

When we talk about exercise, it can sound like a lot of hard work. If we're lounging around on the sofa at the time, the idea of getting out of breath on purpose doesn't sound like much fun. This is a shame, because what we really mean by exercise is *movement*. It's what our bodies are designed to do, after all, and it isn't limited to star jumps in PE lessons or school cross country runs on freezing cold days.

There are limitless ways that we can get active. It goes far beyond taking part in organised sports. From walking to school to kicking a ball about with mates or going wild on the dance floor (or in the kitchen, away from watchful eyes), any kind of energetic activity helps keep us in shape, and not just physically. An active life can provide lasting benefits for our mental health.

☆ **Physical activity can help to clear the mind.** It's a great stress reliever and it also sets us up for a good night's sleep.

 Our brains benefit from an active life. We know that exercise improves blood flow to the brain, improves our memory and concentration and helps keep our brain cells heathy.

 Getting active triggers the release of feel-good natural hormones called endorphins. This is associated with feeling positive and relaxed, which we can consider to be a reward for the mind after putting the body through its paces.

⭐ **An active life can make a positive difference to mental wellbeing.** By building movement into our routines, whether it's a casual stroll or a full-on intense game of netball, we can combine having fun with taking care of both our physical and mental health.

TAKING CARE OF YOUR PHYSICAL HEALTH WILL BENEFIT YOUR MENTAL HEALTH. ♥

Get cracking with creativity

But it's not just about flexing our muscles – it's about flexing
our imagination. That's what being creative is all about. We
don't have to be an amazing artist to be creative – it's very
easy to fall into the belief that our work will be judged, whether
it's a drawing, a short story or a video we've put together and
shared.

This is a shame because what really counts isn't the end result
but the process. I'm certainly no Picasso and I love getting my
creative juices flowing, when making videos and even when
I'm just doodling. No matter what our artistic background or

ability, if something is a fun and rewarding experience and makes us feel good, that can only be a wonderful thing for our mental wellbeing. We might be hankering to learn how to play our favourite song on the guitar, inspired to create a new dance routine or even prefer to keep our creative thoughts private in a journal, but there is a creative outlet that we can all tap into.

Journaling

Keeping a journal is a great way to get creative, be imaginative and write down our thoughts.

We can use journals to write down the things that have gone well or not so well in our week or to note down something we feel grateful for. Not sure where to begin? Just start by jotting down one sentence a day. We can even draw a picture for each day that captures how we're feeling or what we want our day to look like. There's no wrong way to use a journal. We can fill it with stickers, doodles, photos, letters to ourselves, letters to other people . . . . Some people might want to add journaling to their routine too. Perhaps it can be a way to start the day or a way to reflect at the end of it. So forget what people might think. We can keep our journals to ourselves and have fun putting pen to paper – the possibilities are endless! Here are some journal prompts . . .

List five things that inspire or motivate you.

What place makes you feel most peaceful or joyful?

Describe yourself using the first five words that come to mind. Then, list another five words that you'd like to use to describe yourself.

What aspects of your life are you most grateful for?

Describe a choice you regret. What did you learn from it?

☆ Expressing ourselves creatively is known to improve mood and reduce stress. It can also help play a role in the treatment of many mental health conditions such as depression and anxiety.

☆ Using our imagination is a great way to explore difficult or challenging feelings. Some great works of art, including films, songs and video games, ask questions and uncover truths we all recognise about intense emotions like heartbreak, depression, loneliness and anger. In many cases, creativity serves as an emotional pressure release that can also feel rewarding.

☆ Getting creative can help us to meet new people and make friends. Not only can our work invite attention, getting together with others on a project can provide a shared activity that strengthens bonds.

CREATIVITY CAN HELP TO KEEP YOUR MIND IN GOOD SHAPE. ENJOY IT!

My favourite music and films

When I'm missing some creative inspiration or I just want to enjoy a nice afternoon of self-care, I like turning to some of my favourite artists, who have changed my life and mood with their imaginative outlets.

Songs and movies are important to me. They can help me to feel good, make me want to dance and sing, and even be a source of comfort during difficult times. Here are the movies and songs that make my world a better place.

Films

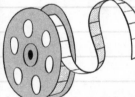

Wonder

The Greatest Showman

Forrest Gump

13 Going on 30

Cheaper by the Dozen

School of Rock

Songs

'Happy' – Pharrell Williams

'Count on Me' – Bruno Mars

'Let It Go' – Frozen

'To Build a Home' – Cinematic Orchestra

'Good Feeling' – Flo Rida

'I'll Be There' – Jess Glynne

'Kill Em With Kindness' – Selena Gomez

We all have personal favourites and guilty pleasures, but if it makes you feel good, who cares, right? Try making your own feel-good playlist, watching list or reading list with all the things that bring comfort and sunshine into your life.

CHAPTER 16

MINDFULNESS, SLEEP ROUTINES AND TAKING CARE

Make it mindful

Mindful is a word we often hear without really understanding what it means. It sounds good, but exactly what does it involve? When someone is being mindful, it means they're focused on the present moment. They're not dwelling on or worrying about something that's happened in the past or what will happen in the future. Instead, they're focused on their surroundings, thoughts and feelings at that moment in time. What's more, whatever's going on, the mindful person simply accepts it for what it is.

Mindfulness is a state of calm that is available to us all. We don't need any previous experience, and with a little practice it can become a lifelong key to mental wellness.

By existing in the present, rather than fretting about past actions or what the future holds, mindfulness can help us to manage difficult feelings like worry, stress and anxiety. In the run-up to exam results, for example, it's easy to feel tense and even lose sleep. The mindful student will remind themselves that they did their best on the day and accept that the results will reflect that. As a consequence, they're free to tune into the present moment to find a sense of calm and acceptance.

We can all be mindful at any time. By following simple techniques, it's something we can call upon during challenging moments or even adopt on a regular basis to help be at peace with ourselves. The great thing about practising mindfulness is that we can do it at any time and place without anyone noticing, be it the local park or in our bedrooms. It's not a song and dance routine but a type of mediation, and it gets easier with practice. Although at first we might feel silly closing our eyes and trying to clear our minds, it can really help us calm down and slow down our racing minds.

We're talking about adopting an outlook on life that keeps things very simple.

There are different ways to embrace mindfulness, but here's a simple strategy that I find effective:

☆ **Focus on breathing.** When we're troubled, anxious or stressed, it's easy for our breathing to pick up the pace without us realising. Reclaim control by concentrating on each breath. Inhale through the nose and gently breathe out through the mouth. Let the air flow naturally and note how that brings a feeling of calm.

☆ **Feel connected.** This is about tuning into our surroundings as well as our inner selves. We should aim to accept whatever we're feeling at the time. Even if we're troubled or stressed, by learning to appreciate what's going on around us in terms of sight, sound, smell, touch and even taste, our minds will begin to calm.

☆ **Accept the moment.** By focusing on our breathing, as well as our thoughts and the world around us, we can begin to feel at peace with ourselves.

☆ **A holiday for the head.** The more we practise being mindful, the easier it becomes. It's a question of training our brains to accept that we can take a break from the noise and pressure of everyday life. Even if we're escaping from a difficult moment or a problem in life, it means we'll return in a better frame of mind to overcome it.

There are all sorts of ways that we can build mindfulness into our lives. The aim is to get our mental health into good shape, and I really believe this should be a fun activity. So to kick things off, I've lined up a selection of ideas . . .

The High Five for a Better Day

This is a technique that encourages us to focus on our five senses (sound, sight, touch, smell and taste) and use them to connect with the here and now. The aim is to consider each one in turn. Then, spend a minute or so tuning out from everything else and just focus on that single, simple and wonderful sensory input.

 What are five things you can see? (For example, a clock on the wall, a flower or passer-by.)

What are four things you can feel? (For example, a phone in your pocket or the seat of your chair.)

What are three things you can hear? (For example, a clock on the wall, birdsong or even just the sound of breathing.)

What are two things you can smell? (For example, flowers, cooking or laundry detergent.)

What is one thing can you taste? (For example, a biscuit or fruit juice.)

The High Five Nature Remix

This is another favourite of mine. It's the same technique as The High Five for a Better Day, but with a focus on the natural world – from the rustle of leaves to the sound of a bird taking flight, from the breeze on our skin to the taste of a freshly picked strawberry. This is a mindfulness exercise we can do when we're out and about that helps us to feel truly grounded.

The Cold Shower Kick-Start

It's really very simple, and although it takes a little courage I urge everyone to try a cold shower! Why? Because standing underneath that icy water – even just for a couple of seconds – sends a direct message to the brain that we need to wake up!

This triggers the release of endorphins, which are the body's natural feel-good chemicals. So, once we're dried off and dressed, we'll feel alert and ready to make the most of the day.

The Body Scan

This is a great exercise for when we've got a lot on our minds. To do it, we need to lie down and pretend our bodies are going through an airport scanner, feet first. Weird, I know, but stay with me. Take a deep breath and try to focus only on the bits of the body that would be passing through the scanner. So first we pay attention to our feet – are they achy, relaxed, tense or comfortable? How do our socks feel against our skin? What happens when we wiggle our toes? Then, as we move through the scanner, focus on the ankles, then the legs, the hips, the stomach, the arms and lastly the head. Take it slowly and really focus on how each part feels. By doing this, we pay attention to every part of the body, staying present and fully checking in with ourselves. It's really relaxing too!

Music for the Soul

As I said before, I love listening to music. When it comes to mental wellness, it's like a natural remedy. Of course, we can listen to great sounds at any time, and there's a song to suit all moods and occasions. Every now and then, however, I find it really helpful to create some time for myself, pop on a pair of headphones and play the most relaxing music I can find. Then, I sit back, close my eyes and breathe slowly and deeply. No matter what's going in my life, it will always take me to a calm, positive space I can call my own.

The great thing about mindfulness exercises is that we can make them up to suit ourselves. Once we've got to grips with the basics and know how to tune into our senses, we can take care of our mental wellness at any time and place – whether we're lounging on the sofa or breathless from running to catch the school bus.

Sleep Zzzzz

Recently, we lived through a time in which it felt like someone had pressed the pause button on everyday life. Lockdown was a response to the Covid pandemic, and it kept us all at home. Overnight, our normal routines disappeared. It's only when we lose something we take for granted that we realise how important it is to us. For many, lockdown showed that we need structure in our days and that routine provides a sense of purpose and control. Following a plan can help us manage uncertainty and stress, and it can lead to a sense of accomplishment. But it wasn't just our daily routines that the pandemic impacted – there are studies that show it disrupted our sleep patterns too. Sleep plays a vital role in our mental and physical wellbeing. It is crucial so that our bodies rest, restore and wake up ready for the next day. Here are some tips for getting a good night's sleep and finding a routine that works for you:

How to Build a Sleep Routine

1. Aim for between eight and ten hours. Everyone is different, but aiming for between six and nine hours every night will benefit both mind and body.

2. Prepare to hit the pillow! Without a little relaxation time before I go to bed, I know I'll struggle to sleep. So I try to wind down for an hour or so beforehand. I'll read a book or maybe soak in a nice hot bath. It means by the time I tuck in, I'm ready to close my eyes. We all enjoy different bedtime routines, and it can become something we look forward to at the end of each day.

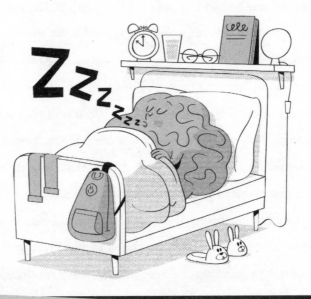

3. Put away your phone. The blue light from our phones can disrupt our sleep pattern, so it's important to put it away before bed.

4. Go to bed and get up at the same time every day. Our natural body clock thrives on routine. As we learn to follow it, we'll get into bed feeling tired, recharge overnight and then rise ready to seize the day.

BUILDING A ROUTINE IS LIKE SETTING DOWN ROOTS. IT ALLOWS YOU TO GROW.

Take care of yourself and others - and shine

So now we've talked about how to build resilience, get active, be mindful and create a sleep routine – but there are some other keys to having better days more often.

We live busy lives, with everyday stresses and worries about things happening all over the world that feel out of our control and can overwhelm us. This means it's important to take care of ourselves and recharge our mental batteries, to allow us to keep moving onwards. I often pencil some relaxation time into my diary and make a date to look forward to. It could be a lazy morning doing nothing and chilling out, starting a new hobby or spending the day with friends watching a movie – anything that will help us relax and take the downtime to unwind.

BE KIND. ALWAYS. YOU NEVER KNOW WHAT SOMEONE ELSE IS GOING THROUGH.

No person is an island. While it's vital to take care of ourselves, we also need to try our best to take care of others – whether this is by being kind and generous to our friends and family or by lending an ear or a shoulder to someone having a tough time. Or even trying to be our best selves in the wider community through gestures like holding the door open for someone or giving up a seat on the bus. It won't earn us any medals, but small actions can have a big impact on the way we feel about ourselves and our place in the world. We can all take the lead in building positivity into our day. And remember, kindness can inspire others to be their best selves and shine too.

Shine on

In my ideal world, all of us would be in tune with our mental health and leading our best lives. That doesn't mean everyone would be permanently smiling without a worry on their mind. In some ways, difficult feelings, setbacks and challenges are part of what makes us human.

What matters is that we're ready to deal with whatever life throws at us so we come through stronger afterwards.

Throughout this book, we've looked at ways to shape our mindset towards a more positive way of thinking. We know that everything from building resilience and routines to making an effort with friends and family can help us to feel good and make meaningful contributions to our world.

With our Lifelines to hand, we're equipped to tackle any mental health issue and seek help when we need it. Even if we feel fine right now, it's always worth keeping those tools to hand. We might thank ourselves one day, or find them useful when it comes to helping someone else.

We've also learned some amazing mindfulness exercises that we can break out at any time and place! From breathing techniques to journaling, doodling or just creating calm, quiet moments within our busy lives, we can build these into our daily routines. The great thing about mindfulness is that we can tap into it on our own, and that might be something that suits lots of people. At other times, getting mindful can be a brilliant way of bringing us all together . . .

My big idea!

We all want to live our best lives, right? At school, the annual sports day is a celebration of movement and physical health. It's good fun and everyone can get involved. Well, wouldn't it be amazing if we could introduce a **WELLNESS SPORTS DAY** to our schools? Think of it as a sports day for the mind, where everyone gets together to have a great time and feel good about themselves. Are we all in? Then here's how to get teachers on board and kick-start a positive mental health movement!

WELLNESS

SPORTS

DAY

☆ **Explain the benefits of mental wellness.** We've seen how important it is to understand our minds and know how to process thoughts and feelings. This is our chance to share that with teachers and bring them on board.

☆ **Suggest a classroom activity.** We need to prove that a mental wellness exercise can help bring a sense of calm and positivity to people. So let's start with small steps and show what a difference it can make in class.

☆ **Take it to the head.** With a class mindfulness activity in the bag, now is the time to go large. Find a good time to speak to the year group tutor or head of school. Then, set out the benefits of a wellness sports day. Be ready to answer any questions and basically inspire them to join the cause.

☆ **Invent events.** Now is the chance to make up games that help us to connect with our minds – like a Mindfulness Marathon or a Sketching Sprint. Take all the fab ideas we've talked about here and turn them into group activities (or sports for the soul!). This is about being creative, enjoying the process and taking pride in the fact that we're striving to make a change for the better.

☆ **Everyone's a winner.** The best thing about a wellness sports day is that everyone can take part. It's not about physical ability or being the best, but a willingness to celebrate a sense of calm. That's available to everyone, including me and you.

Making friends with mental wellness

Luckily, in recent years, a great deal has changed about how we view mental health. We no longer see it purely in terms of problems. We know there are plenty of challenges that can arise when the imaginary levers in our minds work in ways that stop us from feeling ourselves, but mental health is also something to be celebrated. Today, we talk about mental *wellness*, which is a positive state of mind that helps make life shine.

So, as we reach the end of this book, I want us all to rethink our relationship with our heads. It's great to be aware of the challenges and issues that can affect our mental health. Knowledge is power, after all. It means the more we understand about issues such as worry, anxiety, depression, loneliness, grief

and despair, the better prepared we are to recognise the signs and take action at the earliest opportunity. With our Lifelines at hand, we can all look forward to a better day. Why? Because we know that help and support is out there at any time, and we know what steps we need to take to embrace it.

DON'T FORGET TO STOP, LOOK AROUND AND APPRECIATE HOW FAR YOU'VE COME.

At the same time, let's aim to keep our mental health in good shape, just like we do for our bodies. Sport might help us to stay physically fit and healthy, but it's also fun and a rewarding part of life.

We can take the same approach to our minds. It all comes down to checking in with how we're feeling as part of our regular routines. In fact, keeping our mental health in good condition is as simple as brushing our teeth . . .

OK, so reaching for the toothpaste twice a day is something we all have to learn. But eventually, we recognise that the simple act of cleaning our teeth brings lasting benefits. Just think of a smile. It's a natural expression that's freely available to every human being on this planet. It can light up a room, put others at ease or spark laughter and joy. We're talking about a valuable tool that can help us all to feel connected with others.

If we don't care for our teeth, we can become reluctant to show them off. We start to hold back on our smile or hide it behind our hand. In short, it stops us from being ourselves. The way forward? By making dental health part of a daily routine and visiting a dentist for a check-up or at the first sign of a problem, we're free to smile with confidence and crack on with our lives.

Looking after our mental health really can be just as easy. It means learning to check in with our feelings as part of a routine and seeking help for any concerns before they set in. If we can switch on to the fact that our minds shine with a little regular care and attention, just like our physical health, then the prospect of a better day isn't just something we hope *might* happen. It can be a reality for us all.

I ♡ ME.

HELP YOURSELF: RESOURCES

Whenever we board a boat or a plane, we're made aware of what to do in the event of an emergency. There's a good chance we'll never need to put the procedures into practice, and yet it gives us peace of mind for the journey ahead. The same approach applies to good mental health. Even when things are going well and there's no cause for concern, it's always good to know who we can turn to should we need support, help or advice.

It also means we can help those around us when they need it most.

My hope is that in reading this book, you feel equipped for whatever journey life has in store for you next, and that even if you're having a hard time right now, tomorrow will be a better day.

BE YOU.
DO YOU.
FOR YOU.

Samaritans samaritans.org/
Offers listening and support services over the phone or on email to people in need of help.

Childline childline.org.uk/get-support/
Offers a free, confidential service for young people to talk to counsellors via phone, online chat or email.

Hub of Hope hubofhope.co.uk/
A database of local and national mental health support and services.

Mind mind.org.uk/
Provides mental health advice and support, and campaigns to raise awareness and improve services.

CALM thecalmzone.net/
Runs campaigns to raise awareness and challenge the stigma that stops people talking about suicide and asking for help.

Heads Together headstogether.org.uk/
Works to challenge the stigma around mental health and to help people open up and ask for help.

Mental Health Mates mentalhealthmates.co.uk/
A network of peer support groups run by people who are
experiencing their own mental health issues. They meet
regularly to walk, talk and share their experiences without
judgement.

Young Stonewall youngstonewall.org.uk
A dedicated youth team within Stonewall, who campaign
for LGBTQ+ rights and provide information and resources,
including on wellbeing.

The Proud Trust theproudtrust.org/young-people/
Provides help and resources for LGBTQ+ young people.

Switchboard switchboard.lgbt/
Provide support and information via an LGBT+ helpline,
including phone, email and online chat services.

Kids Helpline kidshelpline.com.au/
A free, confidential 24/7 online and phone counselling service
for young people aged five to twenty-five in Australia.

Youthline youthline.co.nz/

Provides support to young people aged twelve to twenty-four in New Zealand, including a 24/7 helpline (via phone, email, text and webchat) as well as free face-to-face counselling, mentoring, and school and community programmes.

The MINDS Foundation mindsfoundation.org/

An organisation based in India which works to remove the stigma around mental health illnesses and improve access to care.

LifeLine South Africa lifelinesa.co.za/

Offers a 24-hour phone counselling service to anyone in South Africa who is struggling, and aims to improve emotional wellness for individuals and communities.

ASKING FOR HELP CAN BE A LIFELINE. NEVER BE AFRAID TO REACH OUT FOR IT.

ACKNOWLEDGEMENTS

Writing this book means so much to me.

I wish I had been able to access the contents of this book when I was at secondary school. I feel like it would have helped me navigate the challenges of growing up and the teenage years. I am so grateful that I have been given the opportunity to write this book; I believe it will help so many young people to weather the storms and find the brighter skies.

Firstly, I must say the biggest thank you to my incredible team at Wren & Rook: Ruth Alltimes, Laura Horsley, Kaltoun Yusuf and Victoria Walsh, as well as the wonderful design team: Samuel Perrett, Pippi Grantham-Wright and Kat Slack.

Matt Whyman has been instrumental in making my thoughts a reality. Thank you, Matt, for helping me to shape my words in the right way and bringing this book to life. Huge thanks also to The Boy Fitz Hammond for his iconic illustrations that add a real edge to the message we are trying to share.

These incredible people have put everything into this, and it's clear to me that the team see how important this book is and how we have the opportunity to improve the lives of our young readers. There is no doubt that everyone has gone over and above on this; I am very proud of what we have done, together.

Carly Cook and Harry Grenville at The Found, my amazing friends and managers, you have done it again! Through the toughest of times we have pulled together to make this book happen. You two are a relentless force and I always appreciate the relationship we have – this is not just work to us, it's more than that. Harry, I know for you that this book is personal; we have worked so hard together on our mental health campaigning and I know how much this means to you. You are a sister to me and I don't know what I'd do without you. Thank you. I must also say a big thank you to Alice Russell – you have been a calm guiding hand through the rough and the smooth; I appreciate you very much and am excited for all that we have to come.

Since *Live Well Every Day* was published, we have seen the addition of a few new team members. Abby, my unflappable assistant, you have literally changed my life. Since you have joined you have brought order to the chaos, ignited a fresh energy within me and made me smile and laugh on a regular occasion. You are a special person. Holly, you came in at a challenging time, with a sense of calm and assuredness that I really needed. Your work ethic and passion for our cause has been a relentless force. You are also one of the kindest souls – please believe in yourself more.

Elliott, my boy, I have loved getting closer to you than ever before. You keep my head level and my heart strong. Thank you. Mam and Dad, you are incredible parents and I am proud to be your son. Never forget that. Although grief never passes, we have so much to be proud of and so much joy to share. Mam, your 'Knit for Mental Health' has raised so much money, connected communities and will help change the lives of people around the country. We always must remember, even if we help one person, we will have done our bit. I love you.

I must take a moment to thank some friends who have been there for me over the last few years. Adam and Emma, who have been just incredible to me, you are such an amazing couple. Adz, your voice and sense of reason has saved me countless times, I will never forget. I am so pleased and honoured you've asked me to be godfather to your impending arrival. I will do my very best. Tom, you have an energy that always lifts me, even when my chin drops down. We laugh and we joke and that humour is my life tonic at times. Sam, thirty-one years later and we are still going strong – thank you, let's enjoy many more.

As I enter my thirties I realise now more than ever that we must embrace life and see each day as a gift. Surround yourself with good people you love and trust. They are the ones who will miss us when we are gone. To everyone who has played a part in my life thus far, whether mentioned directly here or not, thank you.

I started the book with this quote and I am going to end it the same way:

'Life throws us into the deep end at times, however, with the help of family and friends, we overcome even the most seemingly insurmountable challenges.'